Globalisation, Tourism and Simulacra

This book draws on the thought of Baudrillard to explore the effects of globalisation and tourism in a Thai context. Arguing that tourism does not necessarily erode local culture but that local culture can in fact be recreated through globalisation and tourism, the author employs studies of the Damnoen Saduk and Pattaya floating markets, showing them to be simulations of Thai culture that undergo changes of form, cultural content and activity, through various stages of representation. With a focus on the themes of the circulation of value and signs, the play of differences and orders of simulacra, this volume examines the extent to which Baudrillard's theory can apply in a non-western context and in relation to tourism. A study of consumption, tourism and the relations between the global and the local, *Globalisation, Tourism and Simulacra* will appeal to scholars of sociology and geography with interests in tourism, globalisation and social theory.

Kunphatu Sakwit is Lecturer in the Department of Sociology and Anthropology at Chulalongkorn University, Bangkok, Thailand. She obtained a PhD in Sociology from University of Kent, and a Master's degree in Social and Cultural Theory from University of Bristol. She completed her first degree in Political Science, majoring sociology from Chulalongkorn University, Thailand. Her research interests are in Baudrillard studies, postmodernism, sociology of tourism, socioloy of globalisation, critical and social theory, and also risk society.

Routledge Advances in Sociology

For more information about this series, please visit: www.routledge.com/Routledge-Advances-in-Sociology/book-series/SE0511

Globalisation, Tourism and Simulacra

A Baudrillardian Study of Tourist Space in Thailand

Kunphatu Sakwit

LONDON AND NEW YORK

First published 2021
by Routledge
2 Park Square, Milton Park, Abingdon, Oxon OX14 4RN

and by Routledge
605 Third Avenue, New York, NY 10017

First issued in paperback 2022

Routledge is an imprint of the Taylor & Francis Group, an informa business

Publisher's Note
The publisher has gone to great lengths to ensure the quality of this
reprint but points out that some imperfections in the original copies may
be apparent.

British Library Cataloguing-in-Publication Data
A catalogue record for this book is available from the British Library

Library of Congress Cataloging-in-Publication Data
Names: Sakwit, Kunphatu, author.
Title: Globalisation, Tourism and Simulacra : a Baudrillardian Study of
Tourist Space in Thailand / Kunphatu Sakwit.
Other titles: Baudrillardian Study of Tourist Space in Thailand
Description: Abingdon, Oxon ; New York, NY : Routledge, 2021. |
Series: Routledge advances in sociology | Includes bibliographical
references and index.
Identifiers: LCCN 2020014139 (print) | LCCN 2020014140 (ebook) |
ISBN 9780367863043 (hardback) | ISBN 9781003018278 (ebook)
Subjects: LCSH: Tourism–Thailand–Case studies. |
Globalization–Thailand–Case studies. | Markets–Thailand–Case studies. |
Baudrillard, Jean, 1929-2007. Simulacres et Simulation.
Classification: LCC G155.T5 S25 2021 (print) | LCC G155.T5 (ebook) |
DDC 338.4/791593–dc23
LC record available at https://lccn.loc.gov/2020014139
LC ebook record available at https://lccn.loc.gov/2020014140

ISBN: 978-0-367-54001-2 (pbk)
ISBN: 978-0-367-86304-3 (hbk)
ISBN: 978-1-003-01827-8 (ebk)

DOI: 10.4324/9781003018278

Typeset in Times New Roman
by Integra Software Services Pvt. Ltd.

If an exotic place only offers simulation of local culture, will you be interested in going there?

To my lovely family

Contents

Acknowledgements

This book is based on research undertaken at the University of Kent under the guidance of Professor Larry Ray and Dr Vince Miller. I would like to express my most sincere gratitude to them for their guidance, warm encouragement and patience during the course of my studies. Both highly experienced in the field of my research, they have been extremely supportive: I have learnt much through our discussions and through our work together. Again, I am really grateful to Larry and Vince for giving me the chance to grow up. I am fortunate and honoured to have had Professor Jonas Larsen and Dr Dawn Lyon as my PhD examiners. Their challenging, but constructive and meticulous, comments helped to improve my work immensely in preparation for publication. I would also like to thank my editor at Routledge, Neil Jordan, and an anonymous reader for providing an opportunity to write the book and for giving useful feedback. I am indebted to Jean Baudrillard, who was an inspirational social theorist, for his influential and penetrating works.

My PhD was fully funded by The Royal Thai Government Scholarship, and I would like to show my appreciation to The Office of the Higher Education Commission for their financial support. I would like to thank everyone who participated in the interviews and surveys for their generous support during my fieldwork. My special thanks go to Pamela Bertram, who helped me work on the English language. I also would like to thank Professor Jan Pahl for her warm encouragement; Jan is a very lovely landlady and an inspirational woman. I owe a very important debt of gratitude to my family who have been truly supportive of my study. Their advice, as well as encouragement, has been invaluable to me, and without their support and help, I would not have come this far. I would like to thank my friends and PhD colleagues for their honest suggestions; as we always say, 'we are getting there'.

1 Introduction

Prospective tourists may get the impression from the media that the traffic in Bangkok is terrible. The city is large and busy and this is one of the most common images of Bangkok and Thailand. However, the waterways within and outside Bangkok are a unique symbol of the country. As Bodry (2012) states, though Bangkok's usual icons are tuk-tuks and traffic, its waterways are the true symbols of a city that was known as the 'Venice of the East' during much of the nineteenth century. In the capital, they are still used for transportation, providing people with the opportunity to travel by motorboat to many sites around the city. But what was the true importance of the waterways for Thai people? According to Cohen,

> the rivers and canals were the main mode of transportation and a main source of food; on the larger rivers and canals, stores nucleated into markets on water, called Talad Nam in Thai, consisting of land-based Chinese shop houses and Thai farmers floating on boats.
>
> (Cohen 2016, pp. 62–63)

Thus, waterways contributed greatly to the daily life of the local population, with floating markets being a large part of it. Rivers and canals were not only used for transportation, but were also trading places. However, due to a transition from water-bound to land-based motorised transportation and the creation of market facilities along the new land-based routes, waterborne travel and trade in the markets along rivers and canals declined and, in many cases, disappeared (Cohen 2016, p. 63). With road construction and transportation, the Thai way of life changed forever. Pongajarn, Van der Duim and Peters (2016, p. 1) state that following the development of road-transportation systems in the 1950s and 1960s, many floating markets disappeared, although some were relocated as tourist attractions.

Present-day floating markets are not an authentic representation of traditional Thai culture and local way of life, but rather a simulation, displaying an image of the country. Through this careful selection of culture for tourists, Thailand has been able to establish a particular image that may captivate a wide audience and attract visitors. However, it is not the 'Rough Guide' to the real Thailand, but instead a simulation of the country, as a product to be sold to tourists. According to Debbage and Daniels, tourism is not a single product, but a wide range of products and services that interact to provide an opportunity to fulfil the tourist experience that comprises both tangible and intangible products (cited by Judd 2006, p. 325). A combination of various products and services is important for Thailand's tourism, as visitors enjoy Thai food, visiting islands and receiving friendly service from locals.

In 2019, the Tourism Authority of Thailand (TAT) reported that, 'they are expecting 3.18 trillion Baht in overall tourism revenue for the country in 2020, or a 4% year-on-year increase' (TAT News 2019). Thailand has become reliant on tourism-based development, which targets an increase in the number of tourists. Tourism Authority of Thailand recently reported, 'Thailand's quality tourism strategy, which attracts higher quality tourists, has become successful' (TAT News 2017). This is similar to tourism strategies used in other less-developed countries:

> Indonesia, for example, continues to place emphasis on attracting quality tourism, which is conventional tourism in four- and five-star hotels rather than small-scale tourism such as backpackers, and as in many less developed countries the backpacker subsector is ignored.
>
> (Hampton 2003, p. 96)

This is because high-quality tourism seems to generate a larger amount of revenue than small-scale tourism.

A country's tourism is dependent on the flow of capital and international tourist arrivals. Tourism is part of globalisation and vice versa. As a product to be sold to tourists, a place does not inherently become a tourist attraction; rather it is socially created as a tourist attraction. To become a tourist attraction, a local place, or destination country, it needs to reinvent its cultural content as well as tourist-orientated activity.

Thailand has established a reputation for cultural tourism, which is the main focus of this book. Cultural tourism has been promoted for several decades; during the 1980s, 'cultural heritage' appeared to be the promotional catchphrase, as seen during the Bangkok Bicentennial in 1982, when several of the city's monuments were renovated (Peleggi 1996, p. 435). The recent marker of culture tourism in Thailand is 'Thainess'. The Tourism Authority of Thailand (TAT) states that 'Thainess is identified as the unique characteristic of the land, along with the population's strong adherence to traditions that have evolved over more than 700 years, and the remarkable blend of the old and new' (cited by Peleggi 1996, p. 441). Thawatchai Arunyik, governor of TAT, states, 'We launch Thainess to show the Thai way of life and four experiential Thainess products are ecotourism, weddings and honeymoons, health and wellness, and experience of Thainess products, e.g. Thai boxing, Thai cooking classes' (Wood 2013). In this way, the creation of signs and images enables Thailand to become a tourist destination. This also produces cultural value of Thainess and offers an experience of Thai culture for tourists. The emergence of place and the production of cultural value and activity are important steps that may help us understand the effect of globalisation and tourism on the local.

As presented earlier in this chapter, after roads became the main system of transportation in Thailand, floating markets that were once the real, local way of life were reconstructed as tourist attractions. These markets are the case studies of my book, in particular Damnoen Saduak and Pattaya Floating Markets. The social life of local markets is an interesting area of research as the following works indicate: Bestor (2001) proposes that market and place can be connected through the globalisation of economic activity, and yet they are reconnected in different ways; he investigates the interrelatedness of Tokyo's Tsukiji seafood market with other local markets in different places in terms of global flows of economy, information, cultural images and orientations (p. 78). His work shows how global flows make the local place connect to and reconnect with distant others and locates the local market in a broad context.

Regarding the interconnection of the global with the local market, Taylor introduces a 'sensory turn', exploring how 'local culture looks, smells and tastes very different to that which appears in many accounts of interaction between migrants and host communities' in the context of Ridley Road Market, a street market in northeast London (Taylor 2013, p. 1). The differences in feelings, flavours and smells between migrant and host communities foster the interactions between these two groups. Lyon and Back research fishmongers in a south London market using multi-sensory ethnographic research, and they examine how global connections are threaded through the local economy within a landscape of increasing cultural and racial diversity (Lyon and Back 2012, p. 1). Using a multi-sensory approach enables us to perceive the influence of global flows on the local market. However, the effect of global flows may vary according to the local context. In order to contextualise the effects of globalisation and tourism in Thailand, I will only look at floating markets, in particular those of Damnoen Saduak and Pattaya.

Why have these two case studies of floating markets been chosen? According to Cohen,

> The considerable body of sociological and anthropological research on tourism in Thailand has more or less neglected the study of floating markets as a tourist attraction, although these markets have, in the last few years, attracted the attention of mainly Thai researchers from other fields.
>
> (Cohen 2016, p. 60)

In the field of tourism and hospitality management, Wattanacharoensil and Sakdiyakorn (2015, p. 1) explore the potential of floating markets in Nakhon Pathom Province as creative tourism destinations, while Vajirakachon and Nepal (2014, p. 1) examine the processes of engaging the local community in the development and promotion of the Amphawa Floating Market, near Bangkok, as a tourist attraction. Recently, however, there have been two pieces of sociological research on floating markets in Thailand. The first, conducted by Cohen, is a study of the permutations of 21 local floating markets under the influence of tourism, in which he orders the contemporary floating markets into a sequential typology of continuously active floating markets, revived floating markets, new, neo-traditional floating markets and new, innovative floating markets (Cohen 2016, pp. 60 and 65). In relation to my research, Cohen categorises Damnoen Saduak and Pattaya Floating Markets as a revived floating market and new, innovative floating market respectively.

Pongajarn et al. (2016, pp. 1–2) also undertook sociological research on five floating markets in Thailand, including Damnoen Saduak and Pattaya, by using actor-network theory for the method of analysis and investigating how relations between humans and non-humans/objects bring about different paths of development in these floating markets, especially regarding their appearance and reappearance as tourist attractions. These two works run parallel to my study in terms of having chosen Damnoen Saduak and Pattaya Floating Markets as case studies. Additionally, they share a general purpose of study similar to my research, which examines the influence of tourism on the local floating markets in Thailand.

I have been unable to locate sociological studies of floating markets in Thailand that look at signs and cultural simulation, especially signs and the emergence of floating markets as tourist attractions. Also, there is no research on the production of value and the cultural content of the floating markets in Thailand. These are the focus of my research questions which study the ways Damnoen Saduak and Pattaya Floating Markets have become tourist attractions, and the difference between the interpretations of Thai workers and those of tourists in regard to Thai culture.

Regarding social interaction in markets, Watson (2009, pp. 1577 and 1581) explores the multiple forms of sociality that can be observed in eight UK market sites and the potentiality of markets as social space. Different forms of social interaction can occur in a local market. In addition to being a public and social space, interaction between the global and local in Damnoen Saduak and Pattaya Floating Markets can be seen as a reciprocal process, in which global flows reconstruct the floating markets for tourism, while the local places offer differentiated representation of Thai culture to different tourist groupings. The other research question investigates the cultural consequences of globalisation and tourism in Thailand and how interactions between the global and local constitute an experience of Thai culture in the markets. Despite the context of floating markets in Thailand, globalisation and tourism affect simulation of culture differently in each floating market.

I selected these floating markets, rather than looking at other spaces of cultural tourism and globalisation, for example, shops and restaurants, because floating markets are a 'must-do' for tourists in Thailand; they represent their experience of Thailand in general. Floating markets appear on Thailand's tourism websites, as well as in guidebooks, brochures and the media. I concentrated my research on these two floating markets since they are apparently orientated towards foreign tourists, yet display different representations of local Thai culture. Damnoen Saduak Floating Market, which is widely popular among foreign tourists in general, reflects local Thai culture, while Pattaya Floating Market specifically matches Chinese tourists' preferences (see also Cohen 2016; Pongajarn et al. 2016) and only offers simulation of local Thai culture.

Case studies of local floating markets in Thailand

Damnoen Saduak Canal used to be the major transportation route in Ratchaburi Province, as well as its centre of trading. In this case, 'floating market' refers to a type of market where people can exchange, sell and purchase products on water, or it refers to water trading or water market. The Tourism Authority of Thailand (2020) states that the Damnoen Saduak Floating Market has caught tourists' attention as the image of tourism since 1971.

In the past, floating markets constituted the economic activity of local people. The area of Damnoen Saduak is known for the abundance of fruit farming, and the floating market offered local crops and produce such as fruit and vegetables. Being located by the canals, water trading in Damnoen Saduak Floating Market became central to the way of life and culture of local people, yet the old market disappeared because of developments in transportation and road construction. Later, the market was moved across the canal to be close to the main road, so that it was more convenient for tourists travelling there by car.

This market has featured in two famous Hollywood films: the 1974 James Bond film, *The Man with the Golden Gun*, and 2008's *Bangkok Dangerous*, starring Nicolas Cage. The current form of Damnoen Saduak Floating Market differs from the original floating market, since the canal is no longer the main means of transportation in the area. The floating market has also changed in accordance with the needs of tourism, in terms of its purpose, products, pattern of trading and more besides, in order to target tourist arrivals and meet demand.

Damnoen Saduak Floating Market, also known as Khlong Ton Kem Floating Market, has existed for more than 100 years and was the original, traditional floating market where local people came to sell and exchange local produce. It is located in Ratchaburi Province in the west of Thailand, which is about a one-and-a-half-hour's drive (80km) from Bangkok. Tourists can travel there by bus and car. The market covers both sides of the canal, meaning tourists can take a boat ride to look around the market or walk along the canal. If tourists travel to the market with a group tour, tour guides park their cars in the market car park, where tourists can directly board the market's boat services.

Before moving next to the main road, the old floating market used to be run by the local municipals. In about 1972, the Damnoen Saduak Floating Market changed its location from the Ludplee to the Tonkem Canal in order to be accessed by road (Pongajarn et al. 2016, p. 5). Interviewees stated that ownership of the floating market changed after it moved closer to the main road; currently the market is privately owned by boat-service owners who provide this service for tourists visiting the market, with different parts of the market being run by different owners. The services in the market that offer standard prices are Yuwanda Boat Service, Poschawan (J Muay) Boat Service, Paew Boat

Service and Pichai Boat Service. There are 14 other boat services outside the market.

I could not find the exact visitor numbers for Damnoen Saduak Floating Market. Interviewees reported that the market saw a decrease in the number of tourists because they can go to other floating markets in and outside Bangkok. From my observation, the number of foreign tourists outnumbers that of Thai tourists. It is reported that Damnoen Saduak Floating Market used to be a popular destination for Chinese, Japanese, American and European tourists, but the number of these foreign tourists has reduced slightly because the market lacks uniqueness, and many countries have been experiencing economic slowdown (Kao Sod Online 2015).

The floating market has been experiencing a lower turnover than in the previous five to six years due to a decrease in the number of foreign tourists. Products available to buy, on boats and from shop houses, include agricultural products, fruit, vegetables, various souvenir products, clothes, wooden crafts, Thai paintings, souvenir T-shirts, Thai cloth, general Thai food and local Thai food on boats, such as noodles, spring rolls, glass jelly, coffee and Thai tea and fresh coconut juice.

The current floating market is open daily from 8.30am to noon or 1pm. When I conducted interviews, I arrived at the market at 8.30–8.45am. Some shop houses were open and some boat vendors were fixed at the piers. Food stalls and clothes shops on the wooden banks were open in the morning. At 9.00–9.30am, tourists arrived and the market was packed with floating vendors and tourist boats. The noise of boat engines along with people's chatter was loud. The tourist boats were switched on and off as they stopped at vendors and shop houses along the canal. Tourism websites present Damnoen Saduak Floating Market as being the most popular one in Thailand, connecting to the local way of life and offering traces of the traditional water market. Currently, the reinvented Damnoen Saduak Floating Market is one of the most recognisable images of tourism in Thailand.

Unlike Damnoen Saduak Floating Market, Pattaya Floating Market was originally created as a tourist attraction. Officially known as the Pattaya Four Regions Floating Market, it was established as a tourist attraction in 2008 when the owner constructed waterways on a natural swamp to create a floating market. Pattaya city has no history of floating markets or riparian way of life, but instead is famous for its beautiful beaches, variety of entertainment and vibrant nightlife. The Indian travel agency Tripfactory (2017) even describes Pattaya as 'a schizophrenic experience, part package holiday experience, part prostitution central'. Although this area was already popular for its nightlife and various kinds of entertainment, the owner of Pattaya Floating Market introduced his business project as an alternative tourist attraction in Pattaya city, one of culture tourism. The floating market features the Thai architectural style Baan Ruen Thai, or ancient Thai houses and wooden shop houses.

The floating market is located in Pattaya city, Chonburi Province, in the east of Thailand, about a two-and-a-half-hour drive (153km) from Bangkok. Now set over 23 acres (Pongajarn et al. 2016, p. 10), it has gradually expanded over three phases. Tourists can travel to Pattaya by bus and minivan from Bangkok, though the market is not on a list of day trips from Bangkok. Tourists who stay in Pattaya city visit the floating market, with this being sold to tourists as one-day package tour while in Pattaya. Interviewees said most tour groups arrive in the afternoon, having already visited other attractions in Pattaya. The market's main customers are Chinese tourists who come here as part of tour groups, though there are also Thai tourists and some Western tourists. The market has a large car park in front of it. There are different zones in the market – the Southern Zone, Northeastern Zone, Northern Zone and Central Zone – and they indicate activity points in the floating market.

The floating market is privately owned by a Pattaya-based businessman who is a former real-estate businessman and established as Pattaya Four Regions Floating Market Company Limited. After purchasing land situated on a swamp, he reconstructed an attractive pond and floating market. Although it is termed a 'floating market', it is a well-organised place. Interviewees said there are different departments in the market, or company, including marketing, product design, human resources, public relations and market and management positions.

Interviewees state that visitor numbers are normally 5,000–7,000 per day, with Chinese tourists outnumbering other Asian and Thai tourists. They said the foreign-visitor numbers reach up to 10,000 during Chinese New Year and Loy Kratong (a Thai festival in November). In 2014, the market was receiving about 200,000 visitors per month (Pongajarn et al. 2016, p. 10). When I conducted interviews, some interviewees said the number of Chinese tourists decreased because tour agencies experienced problems dealing with the market, especially regarding commission. The types of tourists are mainly Chinese, Asian, Thai and Western.

Some interviewees complained about cheap Chinese tour groups known as Tour Soon Rien, or zero-dollar tours, which they regard as bringing in low-quality tourists who do not have purchasing power. Zero-dollar tours do not benefit the market at all. It refers to tours in which 'Chinese visitors pay Thai-based operators low prices for their package holiday, yet once in Thailand, they are often pressured into buying overpriced food, gifts and accommodation' (Sriring and Temphairojana 2016). It is also reported that 'Thailand's military government says the packages known as zero-dollar tours, aimed at Chinese tourists on a budget, are tarnishing the country's image, and the tourist police have moved to shut them down' (Sriring and Temphairojana 2016). Zero-dollar tours have thus increased Chinese tourist arrivals into Thailand, while simultaneously destroying the country's tourism image. Thailand has gained notoriety for coaxing tourists into buying overpriced items.

Again, I am unable to give the exact turnover rate since it is confidential data. It can be calculated approximately by looking at the number of foreign tourists coming to the market per day, since only foreign tourists have to pay an entrance fee, which is about 200 baht per person (about £5.00). From my interviews, the visitor numbers in Pattaya Floating Market are 5,000–7,000 per day, so the market has an approximate turnover of 1,000,000–1,400,000 baht per day (£25,000–35,000).

Regarding product types, the floating market offers a variety of souvenir products, regional Thai products, souvenir T-shirts, key rings, trinkets, local handmade products (for example, herbal soap), yellow oil and fashionable clothes. The market also has a variety of foodstuffs, such as Thai food, regional Thai food, Thai snacks, Thai desserts, fruit, coffee and Thai tea, as well as an air-conditioned food court in phase 2. There is also a 'Top Shop Zone' in phase 2 and about 500 shops in the whole market. Pattaya Floating Market is open daily from 8am to 8pm. When tourists arrive in the market at the front, they are guided to the entrance gate, where only foreign tourists have to pay for admission fee; entrance is free for Thai tourists. Tourists can walk through different zones of the market or take a boat ride around the market and purchase food and souvenirs. Traders here do not stop tourists to ask them to buy things from their shops; they can walk at ease in the market and watch a cultural show arranged by the market.

Therefore, tourists are able to enjoy not only the floating market, but also entertainment and activities. For example, they can view a herbal garden, a herbal-ball massage demonstration and a monkey show, as well as visit a branch of the Royal Craftsmen College and Agri-nature Learning Centre (Tourism Authority of Thailand 2020). Although there are no floating vendors, vendor boats are stationed by the banks. For Cohen, Pattaya Floating Market is a business enterprise established by a private company and themed as 'old' Thailand, yet still displaying features that disconnect it from Thai traditions (Cohen 2016, pp. 74–75). Pattaya Floating Market appears to be a combination of business and historic culture.

From the two case studies, what is displayed in the two floating markets is only a representation of local Thai culture, which presents a selective image to visitors. Globalisation and tourism foster representation of local places, with the representation of the two floating markets promotes an increase in tourism. What is important here is managing local culture and creating representations that lead to floating markets becoming tourist attractions.

Theoretical framework

Baudrillard is one of the most outstanding postmodern theorists, yet scant attention is paid to Baudrillard's theory in the realm of the sociology of tourism (Rojek 1990, p. 7). Baudrillard's theory relates to tourism, but it is not widely used in the field. Examples of the related books discussing Baudrillard will be presented as follows. Berger (2004) examines cultural perspectives on tourism in the sense that how tourism becomes institutionalised. He uses Baudrillard's simulation and hyperreality to discuss models, and imitations in general (Berger 2004, p. 31). In *Seductions of Place*, Cartier and Lew look at the complexity of touristed landscape formation and different ways that seduction works out in sensory, embodied and emplaced possibilities by developing the themes of the book based on Baudrillard's seduction (Cartier and Lew 2005, pp. 2, 3 and 6). Also related, *Forget Baudrillard?* examines and critically discusses various conceptions of Baudrillard (Rojek and Turner 1993). Rojek and Turner suggest that 'it is symptomatic of the processes of simulation, seduction and hyperreality to which he turns repeatedly in his writings, and the sign economy is the sole universal recognised in Baudrillard's sociology' (Rojek and Turner 1993, p. xii).

Although these are indeed Baudrillard's main preoccupations, Rojek and Turner discuss Baudrillard's ideas as the end of the road; how simulation and seduction cause changes in a variety of social dimensions. However, it seems unclear how the process of simulation is created and maintained. I apply Baudrillard's theory to a non-western context of Thailand, to examine how his conceptions shed critical light on complexity of representation in Thailand's tourism. I show how local Thai culture is reconstructed in globalisation in which packages of Thainess and Thai culture are produced to be sold to tourists in the two floating markets. Looking at both production side and consumption side, my book discusses Baudrillardian concepts including sign value, the system of objects and simulacrum in the sense that these are ongoing stages of representation. These conceptions derive from Baudrillard's 'For a Critique of the Political Economy of the Sign', 'The System of Objects' and 'Simulacrum' respectively. Although these concepts are drawn from different works, they relate to one another. The book is organised by presenting these concepts as a process of constructing complexity of representation. The two floating markets involve stages of representation.

The first stage is the emergence of sign exchange value induced by globalisation and tourism, and this affects the way each floating market becomes a tourist attraction. Then, with circulation of value and signs the cultural contents of the floating markets become non-essentially different, or the places are subject to the play of differential signs. My book then looks at the third stage of representation, orders of simulacra in which activities in Damnoen Saduak and Pattaya Floating Markets move away from reality. Each market enters different stages of simulacrum. I regard simulacrum as the cultural consequence of globalisation and tourism.

Selection of research methods

My book juxtaposes the deductive and inductive approaches. I began my research by exploring a wide range of literature on globalisation and tourism. I found Baudrillard's theories of particular value because he offers insightful and critical view on contemporary society, particularly regarding representation and simulacrum. Baudrillard's theory is therefore, the constant theme of this research. I have engaged only with aspects of the theories that are relevant to the two case studies in this book, referring back and forth to the existing literature and empirical data.

This research was based on interviews with market and associated workers, in order to study and understand different perceptions and interpretation of works in Damnoen Saduak and Pattaya Floating Markets (the production side). To collect data from the workers in those markets, I employed the semi-structured interview. The total number of the interviews was 35; 18 carried out at Pattaya Floating Market and 17 at Damnoen Saduak Floating Market. Fieldwork and interviews of workers in Pattaya Floating Market were conducted from 2 April 2015 to 9 April 2015, while those in Damnoen Saduak Floating Market were undertaken from 30 April 2015 to 8 May 2015.

Contact with the owner of Pattaya Floating Market, was facilitated by one of my father's colleagues. I contacted the owner prior to conducting interviews and asked him for permission to interview workers there. I advised him of the duration of the interviews in advance. The floating market is privately owned by a single owner, so every worker must conform to the regulations of the market. I entered the market as an outsider and researcher, therefore both the owner and the workers understood the purpose of my visit and the purpose of my research. Since I was an outsider, the market arranged for staff members to accompany me during my visit and introduce me to each interviewee. The staff members were not present during the 18 interviews I conducted. Thai people would think it was not their responsibility to answer questions and participate in research unless they had been instructed otherwise. Their only concern is their job and business. The staff arranged for workers who had the time, or were on a break, to meet and talk with me.

Due to it being a well-organised place, I was able to interview members of staff who were working in different positions, including managers, the owner, a vice-president, staff from the marketing and PR departments, the market's guides, staff from the area and product design departments, human resources officers and staff from other positions, such as traders or sellers. Each interview took approximately 30–40 minutes, although some were between 50 minutes and an hour, and all the workers allowed me to voice-record their interview. There was one worker, a trader, whom I approached by myself after my mother bought five scarves from her shop. However, the interview was interrupted as she had to talk to customers when they came in her shop to buy her scarves. During the interviews, I used memo writing to help me memorise key points and important issues. My mother had come prepared with a small token of appreciation for all interviewees, a UV-protection umbrella, which I gave to them on completion of the interview.

In Damnoen Saduak Floating Market, I entered the setting as a researcher. I contacted a key interviewee before proceeding with the interviews so that he could introduce me to other workers. I interviewed market and associated workers, including local authorities, traders, local tour operators, floating vendors, local people and boat vendors, in order to delve into the multiple experiences. These people were involved in tourism of the floating market. However, the workers at this market were unwilling to answer any questions and were suspicious of the research. Some of them said they were too busy, or that they knew nothing, and that I had 'better go and ask others'. Prior to the interviews, I explained the purpose of my visit and research to the workers. When I began to interview them, they said, 'Customers are coming', or 'I'm busy and I don't know anything'. One worker who worked for Paew Boat Service told me he would ask his boss, or the owner, to participate in the interview instead. Market workers were afraid that the interview might be used for other purposes, or thought that I came from other floating markets who they regarded as competitors.

The current incarnation of Damnoen Saduak Floating Market is run by different private owners of boat services, and each part of the market belongs to different owners. The boat vendors, who are employed by the boat-service owners, are paid daily, and the stall traders pay rent to the boat-service owners that they work with. Stall traders and floating vendors needed to have a good relationship with their employers so that they could work at the market. Conducting interviews here was more challenging than in Pattaya Floating Market, and I found it very difficult to approach workers since it was obvious that they did not want to talk to me. They stated that it was a 'waste of their time'. I approached some of the workers by purchasing souvenirs and other items from their shops, during which transactions they would begin to talk and answer my questions.

Some of them objected to being voice-recorded, as they thought the interview might affect the market or their jobs, as they were afraid of the boat-service owners. I conducted some interviews with floating vendors and boat rowers while I was being paddled around the market. The noise of the boat engine[1] and general crowd chatter inhibited to conversation meant that I was unable to record all of the interviews. Instead, as much as I could, I tried to make notes of the answers, words, sentences and the key points that workers talked about, asking them to repeat their answers if I was unsure about their replies. I conducted 17 interviews with workers and gave them a UV-protection umbrella after each interview.

All the interviews were conducted in Thai, except for two interviews with informants in Pattaya Floating Market that were conducted in English. I translated the other interviews from Thai into English. I encountered some difficulties in translation due to language issues. In Thai, we seldom use passive voice, and do not change verbs according to different tenses. We simply use adverbs to show different tenses, for example, we say '47 years ago people 'use' boat as the main mode of transportation. Whereas, in English, passive voice is often used in both spoken and written languages. When translating from Thai to English, I thought I should use active or passive voice. The translators helped me with this. Also, I was not sure how to say some words in English, for example, 'Rok Tang Mo' in Thai means watermelon stall. But, when translating into English, I said 'the place offered watermelon'.

Concerning the word 'Thainess', there is a Thai equivalent to the concept of Thainess that has the same connotations – 'kwam pen Thai' or 'wi ti Thai'. It means the uniqueness of Thailand, Thai way of life and Thai culture. I did not translate this word from Thai. But this word, originally in English, was created and used by Tourism Authority of Thailand and a worker in Pattaya Floating Market. Workers in Pattaya Floating Market used the same word in Thai. It means the same as 'Thainess'. At Damnoen Saduak Floating Market, the market workers described the place as representing original Thai culture, local Thai culture or the Damnoen way of life rather than Thainess. The original floating market signified the uniqueness of Thai culture.

In order to process and analyse interview data, I undertook content analysis in which coding is the necessary first step. I used two types of coding: theory-driven code and data-driven code. Attride-Stirling (2001, p. 390) suggests that 'devising a coding framework can be done on the basis of the theoretical interests guiding the research questions, on the basis of salient issues which arise in the text itself, or on the basis of both'. I undertook coding based on the theoretical framework and recurrent issues in the data, whereby I could examine theory by relating data to the theoretical interests, and this analytical tool was also open for themes directly emerging from the data. There were two cycles of coding.

The first cycle of coding aimed to identify the important key words in the interviews. I started analysing data by transcribing and translating the first five interview transcripts regarding each floating market, and by highlighting all the key words in each answer and question. I wrote down codes that emerged from recurrent issues and highlighted text or sentences that related to predefined codes. After that, I transcribed and translated the rest of the interviews. I also highlighted the key words that arose during the interviews. Some new codes arose in the text, while some resembled those in the first five interviews. Most codes were derived from the written text in the transcriptions, yet some codes were pre-established, namely changes in the floating markets, contrived culture and cultural performance in front of tourists.

Next, I undertook the second cycle of coding, which was the codifying of the interview transcripts, sentence by sentence, to further discover theory-driven codes and data-driven codes. I matched the codes with other segments of data in order to see the consistency of the codes, and to allow other codes to emerge. The second cycle of coding enabled me to develop categories from the coded data and compare them to those that emerged from the first cycle of coding. The two cycles of coding warranted the accuracy of the data analysis and reflected firm patterns in the data. The next stage is to 'distinguish themes from coded text segments, whereby we need to go through the text segments in each code and extract salient and significant themes in the coded text segments' (Attride-Stirling 2001, p. 392). I extracted the salient sub-themes in the coded text segments; sub-themes that were relevant to one another will be presented in the same chapter, such as simulacrum and globalisation. These steps helped me examine the relationship between the theoretical framework and the data.

Apart from interviews, documentary research and qualitative survey were used to study tourist perceptions and experiences of the floating markets. One aspect of Thai culture is that people have consideration for other people's feelings. I wanted to talk to tourists, yet I was very considerate. I did not want to bother them while they were sightseeing at the floating markets. Thai people regard foreign tourists as important guests. Also, I felt a bit awkward and shy about approaching foreigners and stopping them for an interview. Many tourists were wary of Thai strangers who approached them on street in case they turned out to be robbers, illegal tour guides, taxi drivers or even prostitutes. I did not interview tourists, for the tourists who visited the two markets were from different countries. For example, most tourists in Pattaya Floating Market were Asian and therefore might not have been able to speak English fluently, if at all. Although many tourism researchers have carried out interviews with tourists in other contexts, for example Turkey (Haldrup and Larsen 2010) and India (Edensor 1998), there is a difference between conducting research in the context of Thailand and in the context of other places, and between a Thai researcher and a foreign researcher. Tourists would be very wary of speaking with Thai strangers. My experience of approaching tourists in Khao San Road in Bangkok during my pilot study was that most refused to talk to me, saying, 'Sorry, I didn't have time?'.

Therefore, I thought documentary research and surveys would be an appropriate technique for studying their perception of the floating markets without causing them any inconvenience. Documentary research enabled me to access tourist accounts of Damnoen Saduak and Pattaya Floating Markets without bothering them during their tours in the markets. It also meant their accounts were not framed by any questions. For documentary research, the TripAdvisor website was researched to study tourist perceptions of the floating markets, with attention being paid to what they consumed in the markets, how the markets related to Thai culture and so on. TripAdvisor is one of the best-known tourism websites, on which tourists can share experiences with one another and learn about different destinations. I selected the 30 most recent reports of each market on TripAdvisor, and the total number of selected TripAdvisor comments was 60. I conducted documentary research on TripAdvisor by retrieving and analysing comments on Damnoen Saduak and Pattaya Floating Markets that were posted between 4 April 2015 and 20 June 2015.

Data collected from TripAdvisor only represents the perception and interpretation of the tourists who were able to speak English, while excluding non-English-speaking tourists. I used content analysis as the method of analysis. For TripAdvisor, data were available in English text. Most were data-driven codes, with only a few of them being predefined codes, namely Thai culture, experience and perception, which enabled me to see to what extent the findings were relevant to the theoretical framework and to the research questions. I applied content analysis and printed out 30 comments on each market, codifying the data by highlighting key words and phrases in each post before writing them down next to each comment blog.

I then separated the pre-established codes from those that directly emerged from the data, and did this sentence by sentence, for most of the comments were not too long – 'Having devised a coding framework, the codes should be employed with the textual data to dissect it into text segments' (Attride-Stirling 2001, p. 391). I applied both pre-established and data-driven codes to the data and dissected them into text segments. The salient sub-theme of impression was extracted from the coded text segments and regrouped under the theoretical theme. This ensured that the coded data, sub-theme and theme could refer back to the theoretical framework and were relevant to the research questions.

I also conducted qualitative survey interviews to see how foreign tourists interpret floating market with regards to Thai culture. I decided to do this after completing my documentary research. This technique was used to supplement the data from TripAdvisor. As stated previously, there is a difference in carrying out research in the context of Thailand between Thai and foreign researchers. From my experience of the preliminary research, tourists were much more wary about talking to Thai people and would give me a suspicious look when I approached them about taking part in an interview. To avoid the problem, I conducted short surveys with foreign tourists who stayed in the Khao San Road area, a place in Bangkok that is popular with backpackers. It is also a place where many tour itineraries start, some of which are operated by the local hotels. They are able to offer tailor-made packages to suit tourists' needs, such as half-day tours to places outside Bangkok, day package tours and package tours to the south or north of Thailand.

To gain access to tourists on the Khao San Road, it was necessary to have a connection with the hotels, tour agencies and tour guides in order to get permission to distribute the survey interview forms to tourists. I had heard that hotels and tour guides here are not welcoming to Thai tourists or Thai people. My father introduced me to the owner of two hotels in the area: Buddy Lodge, centrally located on Khao San Road, and Hotel De Moc, a ten-minute walk from Khao San Road. My father contacted the owner and I made an appointment to meet him. Then I went to Hotel De Moc to meet him, which is when I asked for his permission to distribute the survey forms.

I entered the setting as a PhD researcher and made the hotel staff aware of the purpose of my study. The owner asked the hotel receptions to distribute the survey interview forms to tourists who checked in and out of the hotels. Similar to documentary research, the survey data showed the experiences of floating markets of English-speaking tourists while excluding other groups. This is because the survey was conducted in English. I left the survey interviews at the hotels and returned about two weeks later to collect them. There were eight semi-structured interview questions, and tourists could write their answers under the questions. The timing of the research was 25 July 2015 to 31 August 2015. The total number of short surveys was 36. I divided the questions into two categories: 'Been to floating markets' and 'Never been to floating markets'.

To analyse data collected from surveys, I undertook content analysis. Similarly, I started with coding, including theory-driven code and data-driven code. I matched the codes with those text segments where the segments became descriptions of the codes. I then extracted sub-themes from the coded text segments and matched the sub-themes with the theoretical framework. Pseudonyms for each participant were used in the research in order to protect the participants' anonymity.

Structure of the book

This book consists of eight chapters, including the introduction. Baudrillard's theory is employed in each chapter. Differences between Damnoen Saduak and

Pattaya Floating Markets will be presented in each analytical chapter on the basis of relevant themes and theory. What follows the introduction is a review of the literature of globalisation, looking at the apparatus of globalisation depending on causal factors, generalised impacts and the binary opposition of the global and local. In Chapter 3, literature on tourism will be discussed, and how different processes in tourism have created Thailand's floating markets.

Chapter 4 introduces Baudrillard's theory and the concepts that will be used and developed throughout the book. This includes discussions of Baudrillard in the context of globalisation, tourism and related themes of the empirical chapters, along with relevant literature. The chapter will also present critiques of his work.

The next three chapters are thematic and analytical, and incorporate data taken from in-depth theoretical analysis. Each chapter shows how the floating markets develop into simulacra and move away from reality; additionally, they each discuss the limitations of working with Baudrillard's ideas. Chapter 5 presents the first theme of the research, namely circulation of value and signs, focusing on the form of the floating markets and looking at how they are tourist attractions.

Due to the flow of capital, together with the flow of tourism, Damnoen Saduak and Pattaya Floating Markets appear to be tourist attractions. Exchange-value takes the form of use-value. Local people set the scene of the floating markets in order to attract tourists and earn a living. The floating markets involve circulation of value and signs, where commodity sign-value legitimises use-value and exchange-value. The tourist-orientated floating markets are commutable with a combinatory system of signs.

Chapter 6 highlights the second theme of the research, which is the play of differences. This chapter looks at the cultural content of the floating markets. Baudrillard's theory on the system of objects will be used to challenge Ritzer's criteria of something form/nothing form. There is no fixed criterion for differentiating unique cultural content from generic cultural content. This is because the cultural contents of the places become non-essentially different. The cultural contents of the floating markets do not depend on functional essence.

Chapter 7 describes final theme of the research, which looks at action in the floating markets. The cultural consequences of globalisation make the floating markets enter different orders of simulacra. Damnoen Saduak Floating Market involves the first order of simulacrum, whereby the place is counterfeit and a reflection of the original local Thai culture. Pattaya Floating Market, meanwhile, changes from a series object in the second-order of simulacrum, presented in Chapter 8, to the model in the third-order of simulacrum. It generates a variety of social forms. Thai culture can make sense only when it accords with the models of the floating market. Action in Pattaya Floating Market makes local Thai culture move further away from reality.

Chapter 8, the conclusion, restates all of the important points of each chapter. It restates the contribution to knowledge. It also presents the implications and limitations of the book and makes some suggestions for future research on globalisation and tourism.

Note

1 In Damnoen Saduak Floating Market, some workers use rowing boats, while others use motorboats, especially for taking tourists around the market. The noise of the boat engine was very loud.

References

Attride-Stirling, J. (2001). Thematic Networks: An Analytic Tool for Qualitative Research. *Qualitative Research*, 1(3), 385–405.

Berger, A.A. (2004). *Deconstructing Travel Cultural Perspectives on Tourism*. Walnut Creek, CA: Altamira Press.

Bestor, T.C. (2001). Supply-Side Sushi: Commodity, Market and the Global City. *American Anthropologist*, 102(1), 76–95.

Bodry, C. (2012). Exploring Bangkok's Canals. *BBC* [Online]. Available from: www.bbc.com/travel/story/20120827-exploring-bangkoks-canals. [Accessed 18 January 2018].

Cartier, C. and Lew, A.L. (2005). *Seductions of Place: Geographical Perspectives on Globalisation and Touristed Landscapes*. Abingdon: Routledge.

Cohen, E. (2016). The Permutations of Thailand's 'Floating Markets'. *Asian Journal of Tourism Research*, 1(1), 59–98.

Edensor, T. (1998). *Tourists at the Taj: Performance and the Meaning at a Symbolic Site*. London: Routledge.

Haldrup, M. and Larsen, J. (2010). *Tourist, Performance and the Everyday: Consuming the Orient*. Abingdon: Routledge.

Hampton, M. (2003). Entry Points for Local Tourism in Developing Countries: Evidence from Yogyakarta, Indonesia. *Geografiska Annaler*, 85B, 85–101.

Judd, D.R. (2006). Commentary: Tracing the Commodity Chain of Global Tourism. *Tourism Geographies*, 8(4), 323–336.

Kao Sod Online (2015). Uniqueness Disappears. Damnoen Saduak Floating Market Saw a Decrease in Visitor Numbers and Slow in Trade. *Prachachart Turakit Online* [Online].

Lyon, D. and Back, L. (2012). Fishmongers in a Global Economy: Craft and Social Relations on a London Market. *Sociological Research Online* [Online]. Available from: www.socresonline.org.uk/17/2/23.html [Accessed 10 February 2018].

Peleggi, M. (1996). National Heritage and Global Tourism in Thailand. *Annals of Tourism Research*, 23(2), 432–448.

Pongajarn, C., Van der Duim, R. and Peters, K. (2016). Floating Markets in Thailand: Same, Same, but Different. *Journal of Tourism and Cultural Change*, 16(2), 109–122.

Rojek, C. (1990). Baudrillard and Leisure. *Leisure Studies*, 9(1), 7–20.

Rojek, C. and Turner, B.S. (1993). *Forget Baudrillard?* London: Routledge.

Sriring, O. and Temphairojana, P. (2016). Thai Crackdown on 'Zero Dollar' Chinese Tour Hits Golden Week. *Reuters* [Online]. Available from:www.reuters.com/article/us-china-tourism-goldenweek-thailand/thai-crackdown-on-zero-dollar-chinese-tours-hits-golden-week-idUSKCN1270Q3 [Accessed 11 March 2018].

Taylor, A.R. (2013). *The Essences of Multiculture: A Sensory Exploration of an Inner-City Street Market* [Online]. Available from: http://research.gold.ac.uk/8359/1/essences%20pre-proof.pdf. [Accessed 10 February 2018].

Tourism Authority of Thailand Newsroom (2017). *Thailand's Strategy to Target High Quality Tourists Pays off* [Online]. Available from: www.tatnews.org/thailands-strategy-target-high-quality-tourists-pays-off/. [Accessed 29 July 2017].

Tourism Authority of Thailand Newsroom (2019). TAT Targets 3.18 Trillion Baht in Tourism Revenue for Thailand in 2020 [Online]. Available from: www.tatnews.org/2019/12/tat-targets-3-18-trillion-baht-in-tourism-revenue-for-thailand-in-2020/. [Accessed 18 February 2020].

Tourism Thailand (2020). *Pattaya Floating Market Trading Centers, Shopping and Floating Market* [Online]. Available from: https://www.tourismthailand.org/Attraction/pattaya-floating-market [Accessed 23 April 2020].

Tourism Thailand Organisation (2020). *Damnoen Saduak Floating Market* [Online]. Available from: https://www.tourismthailand.org/Attraction/damnoen-saduak-floating-market [Accessed 23 April 2020].

Tripfactory (2017). *Exotic Thailand – Luxury. Day Wise Itinerary* [Online]. Available from: www.tripfactory.com/package/exotic-thailand—luxury-406705 [Accessed 2 May 2017].

Vajirakachon, T. and Nepal, S. (2014). Local Perspectives of Community-Based Tourism: Case Study from Thailand's Amphawa Floating Market. *International Journal of Tourism Anthropology*, X(Y), 1–15.

Watson, S. (2009). The Magic of the Marketplace: Sociality in a Neglected Public Space. *Urban Studies*, 46(8), 1577–1591.

Wattanacharoensil, W. and Sakdiyakorn, M. (2015). The Potential of Floating Markets for Creative Tourism: A Study in Nakorn Pathom Province, Thailand. *Asia Pacific Journal of Tourism Research*, 21(S1), 1–27.

Wood, A.J. (2013). TAT Action Plan: 'Higher Revenue through Thainess'. *Eturbonews* [Online]. Available from: https://eturbonews.com/70564/tat-action-plan-higher-revenue-through-thainess [Accessed 22 February 2017].

2 Revisiting globalisation

Introduction

Globalisation is an established area of research and there is a variety of theories addressing it. Globalisation can be perceived from different angles. No theory can claim that totality of globalisation exists. Globalisation varies in different contexts. The wider range of globalisation literature will be discussed. This will enable us to see the effects of globalisation on the local in general, and to critically understand globalisation. The purpose of this chapter is not to refute the existing literature, although I would like to present the old story in a new way.

Although existing globalisation literature offers us a good understanding of the global phenomenon, it might be insufficient for exploring the complexity of social events. What constitutes globalisation is still unclear. To better study the complexity of the globalisation phenomenon, we need to understand how it is constituted. I suggest that globalisation refers to a complexity of social dimensions. In contemporary globalisation, we are unable to separate one social dimension from another. This is because all social dimensions implode. Globalisation is a multidimensional phenomenon and its structural forms vary according to different contexts.

There are three points to be addressed in this chapter. First, globalisation theories seem to consist of a one-size-fits-all approach, which refers to causes of globalisation. Second, globalisation triggers changes in social processes, which refers to a generalised impact of globalisation. Third, the idea of the local is an alternative to globalisation.

Globalisation according to a one-size-fits-all approach

Much of the globalisation literature reduces globalisation to either single or multiple causes, especially economic reductionism. The globalisation literature uses an approach that proposes that the economic system affects the emergence of globalisation, for example:

Harvey's conception of globalisation offers us a wide-angle view of the evolving geography of globalisation. He introduces time-space compression and characterises capitalism as the acceleration of the pace of life, overcoming spatial barriers, with the result that the world seems to have imploded upon us (Harvey 2001, pp. 240–298). Capitalism, accompanied by time-space compression, affects our way of life, although the time-space relationship hardly matters in this era of contemporary globalisation. For example, a British client of the UK's bank is able to manage his own banking account via the internet banking system no matter where he is, and so the expansion of capitalism renders spatial barriers irrelevant.

Capitalism and time-space compression precede globalisation, with the system of accumulation facilitating the extension of social relations. Harvey's idea is an economically driven approach to capture social change. For him, the shift in social relations, along with the expansion of capitalism, homogenises a world that is shrinking. In this case, globalisation is accorded a greater global, as opposed to local, extent in which globalisation relates to the expansion of the capitalist system, which imposes on the local context. Although capitalism is associated with the spread of globalisation, economic factors do not function alone. Looking back at the example of the bank customer stated above, flows of capital and the expansion of capitalism rely on development in communication technology. This enables the bank's clients to access and manage their accounts online, regardless of place and time.

Further, capitalism does not evenly affect locality. For instance, Superdry clothes sold in the UK are made in India because of the cheap labour costs. It was reported that the British company was exploiting factory workers in India in order to maximise profit, with workers being paid as little as 28p per hour and having to work in sweltering conditions in order to meet unrealistic targets (Flynn 2015). Different localities seem to unevenly and unfairly benefit from the global market because of their social and geographical context. In this way, the apparatus of globalisation does not only depend on an economic approach, but also the local context.

Some of the most debated works on globalisation centre on three schools of thought: globalism, scepticism and transformationalism. However, this section will only focus on the first two. Proponents of these regard the global economy as the main driving force of globalisation. Globalists propose that the present global capitalist economy, which is different from that of the previous era, has been transformed into the era of the weightless economy (Held and McGrew 2002, pp. 52–53). Globalists introduce an economic approach for studying the global phenomenon, by which they perceive the influence of the global capitalist economy as unprecedented. Globalists additionally assert that both productive and financial capital have been liberated from national and territorial constraints, and markets have become globalised to the degree that domestic economies have had to adapt to global competitive conditions (Held and McGrew 2002, p. 53).

Therefore, the first group see the weightless economy, along with the liberation of financial capital, as the cause of globalisation. Alternatively, sceptics think that the current international economy is not new, and national boundaries still matter in the world economy. Hirst and Thompson contend that,

> The present highly internationalised economy is not unprecedented, rather it existed before as one of a number of distinct conjunctures of the international

economy, and most companies are based nationally, and the globalised economy is an open world market relied on by trading nations.

(in Held and McGrew 2000, pp. 68–75)

The emergence of globalisation is the consequence of a transnational economy, and the global economy is dependent on trading nations. Thus, globalists note the unprecedented transnational economy causes de-territorialisation, while sceptics believe that the international economy is based upon nation states. An important thing is that globalisation cannot be reduced to economic factors. Flow of capital and the expansion of the market are, to some extent, subject to political regulation and agreement among trading nations.

Some theorists speak of a political factor. Scholte (2002, p. 26) argues, 'Little if any territoriality today exists independently of supraterritoriality. Most contemporary regional, national, provincial and local conditions co-exist with – and are influenced by – global circumstances'. Indeed, territoriality is changed by its encounters with supraterritoriality (Scholte 2002, p. 26). Any territoriality hardly exists independently of supraterritoriality. The expansion of the global economy, as well as supraterritoriality, is one of the preceding events and conditions of globalisation, where globalisation is the outcome of the global market and global politics.

Unlike the aforementioned theorists, some use a cultural approach to capture globalisation. The term hybridisation is used to denote the culture of globalisation. In this process, the meanings of externally originating goods, information and images have been 'reworked, syncretised and blended' with existing cultural traditions and forms of life (Featherstone 1995, pp. 116–117). The cultural blend, the mixture of different cultures, is a precondition of globalisation. Wang and Yueh (2005, p. 188) note hybridity as the generation of new ways in which to understand and produce possible new cultures. 'The hybridisation thesis states that cultures borrow and incorporate elements from each other, creating hybrid forms' (Holton 2000, p. 140). Hybridised culture refers to the interpenetration of one culture into another. This facilitates the spreading of globalisation. One culture mixes with another culture so as to create a new cultural form, or cultural blend. For hybridised culture, therefore, national boundaries are irrelevant, and locale is not constitutive in globalisation.

In addition, Hannerz (2004, p. 249) talks about cosmopolitan inclinations that aim to make selective use of their habitats to maintain their expansive orientation towards the wider world and sees today's cosmopolitans and locals as sharing common interests in order for cultural diversity to be able to survive. The term 'cosmopolitanism' differs from 'hybridised culture'; the former widens opportunity for people in different places to receive other cultures, whereas the latter, a cultural consequence, is the mixture of one culture with others that generates a new cultural outcome. Although they are different terms, people situated in one place can experience both, as seen in the example of Thai food in the UK. British people are able to have Thai food in their home country (cosmopolitanism), yet it might not be authentically Thai, as the taste of the food is adapted in order to suit British people (hybridisation). Therefore, cosmopolitanism and hybridisation both affect the circumstances of people's lives.

When local people become de-traditionalised and free to adapt to other cultures, cosmopolitanism can assist locals in adhering to their own culture; cosmopolitanism places value on diversity, since it cannot exist without locals and vice versa (Hannerz 2004, p. 249). Cosmopolitanism is thus the incorporation of the global into the local, and the adaptation of the local to global culture. 'Global culture that is not tied to any place or period refers to standardised commodities, generalised human values and a uniform scientific discourse of meaning operating at several levels simultaneously' (Smith 1990, pp. 176–177).

Global culture relates to standardisation processes that traverse national boundaries whereby global and local components are interwoven with each other. For global culture, the differentiation of the global from the local might not be clear. The following are examples of global culture: a special menu choice of Kentucky Fried Chicken (KFC) in Thailand is Kao Yum Kai Sab (spicy Thai rice with spicy fried chicken); another example is that MTV Thailand shows a variety of foreign and Thai-genre music. At first glance, KFC and MTV seem to have been standardised in global culture, but they have not. They become adapted by the local context. The spread of global culture, to some extent therefore, is subject to local context. Also, the prevalence of global culture varies according to local contexts. It may become widely accepted in one context, whereas it may have a low impact on other locales.

Global culture and hybridisation are not independent processes, whereby the spread of global culture is, to some extent, associated with the expansion of the capitalist system. The economic system is the precondition of global culture. Looking back at those examples, transnational companies (KFC and MTV) facilitate the spread of global culture and vice versa. There is no boundary between economy and culture in globalisation. As well as these approaches, Castells (2010, pp. 13–52) appears to emphasise that information and technological development are the principal causes of globalisation, 'The information-technology revolution has restructured the capitalist system, and the internet, along with new developments in telecommunications, have led to a major technological shift from decentralised to pervasive computing'.

In this case, the emergence of globalisation relates to development in technology communication which expands social networks and the capitalist economic system across time and space. In contrast to mono-causal theories, still others argue that globalisation is a multi-dimensional phenomenon. Unlike globalists and sceptics, transformationalists connote globalisation as moving ahead at unprecedented levels in recent times, and that globalisation might have a differentiated effect, depending upon the dimension (economy, politics, culture and so on), or location, wherever it is experienced (Martell 2007, p. 4). Stances taken by transformationalists' concern multidimensional globalisation that can produce different effects. As a multi-causal phenomenon, globalisation can extend its effect to many different locales. However, transformationalists do not further elaborate on the intermingling of social dimensions.

To look at this more closely, Appadurai highlights the interplay between different social dimensions, and theorises global cultural flow as disjuncture. He depicts the new global cultural economy as complex, overlapping and disjunctive by introducing the framework of five landscapes – ethnoscapes, technoscapes, financescapes, mediascapes and ideoscapes – along with disjunctive relationships among these dimensions of global cultural flows (Appadurai 1996, pp. 33–36). Multiple imagined worlds are created by the historically situated imaginations of persons and groups. Appadurai's concept of disjuncture enables us to see complicated configurations of globalisation, and to unfold other social forces behind this global phenomenon. The spread of globalisation depends on the overlapping of the five landscapes.

The multi-causal factors, including the transnational movement of people, financial flows, the media, technology development and the spreading of global ideology, are not new, they already exist in the capitalist system. These are important causes of globalisation, yet they do not make globalisation become something in itself. Instead, the spread of globalisation is dependent upon these causal factors and the interplay between them. In regard to these mono-causal and multi-causal factors, have we ever doubted that globalisation actually exists?

Rosenberg (2005, pp. 6–22) argues that globalisation is not a process *sui generis* that is misunderstood by globalisation theories as having both the direction and momentum of a historical process. 'This is a historical process that Marx already identified as the spreading scope and volume of transnational relations, which is technologically orchestrated and depends on spatio-temporal integration according to the "laws of the motion of capitalist development"'.

For Rosenberg, what is termed globalisation is the same process, that brings about transnational relations, as capitalism, and therefore globalisation might not even exist. He also outlines 'the problem of globalisation' along with social theory as follows: Globalisation in itself does not connote any particular kind of society, it is simply a process of spatial expansion and integration; moreover, it incorporates a social theory drawn from elsewhere to provide the explanation for large-scale social change (Rosenberg 2005, pp. 11–13).

Rosenberg's work enables us to undertake critical inquiry into globalisation theory. According to this view, globalisation does not inherently happen, but its appearance depends on the spatial expansion of capitalism. However, he overestimates the uniformity of globalisation; he sees capitalist development as uniform, as in worldwide spatial expansion and integration, but he does not pay attention to its different impacts upon each locality. As stated previously, the economic factor does not function alone. Rather, it is affected by other social dimensions and the local context. For example, Western countries benefit from the global economy to a higher degree than African countries, and different locales are not evenly integrated into capitalism. What is termed as global therefore, does not imply uniformity.

Instead, what constitutes globalisation is contingent upon different local contexts. The effect of spatial expansion and incorporation varies with different locales.

Rosenberg's main problem is that he overlooks the dynamics of globalisation, especially the interaction between the global and the local, and the interplay between one social event and another. This might be the reason why he claims globalisation does not actually happen. The second problem, in which globalisation integrates with other social theories drawn from elsewhere, is unsurprising, as there is no single way to theorise and fully understand globalisation, as most theorists connect globalisation with other events. Other systems, including modernity, capitalism and spatial-temporal reconfiguration, all result, to some extent, from the emergence of the apparatus of globalisation.

Brown (2008, pp. 42–43) proposes that 'globalisation is entirely what we make of it, in that globalisation appears as many things with various manifestations, meanings, connections and interrelated complexities'. The complexity of social events fosters the existence of globalisation. Globalisation does therefore happen somewhere, and it can exist in a variety of social forms. In this way, what is termed globalisation is a consequence of other social events, or the effect of globalisation varies when applied to different contexts. Again, globalisation is not an independent process, but is created socially.

The homogenised effects of globalisation: globalisation as a social process

This section presents theories that view globalisation as a process, which is a generalised impact of globalisation. I will begin this section by presenting Giddens' work. He regards globalisation as restructuring the ways in which we live in a profound manner, and it is a truly global reduction in everyday life in which affects the intimate and personal aspects of our lives, especially traditional family systems (Giddens 2002, pp. 4–12). For Giddens, globalisation reshapes our everyday life. It affects individuals and family life, for example, social identity no longer has binding restrictions to family and tradition, and most people who tend to be exposed to multiple choices freely choose their identity. People do not strongly connect to tradition and family; instead, these turn out to be choices for individuals. This is because people are bound to the influence of global flows and global culture. For instance, some Thai families raise their children in a Thai-Western style, and usually send them to study at international schools, or to study bilingual programmes (English-Thai), from which they can learn about Thai and Western cultures. Due to the prevalence of Western culture and values, Thai students are taught to express their opinions and engage in discussions, whereas previously, arguing and disagreeing with teachers was deemed unacceptable.

Giddens suggests that it is important to look at the relationships between micro and macro that permeate one's personal life, along with global life and institutions, that are very much connected with each other through globalisation (Giddens in Rantanen 2005, p. 65). Globalisation causes a change in social process, whereby one's personal life and global institutions become more interrelated than they previously were. What constitutes social identity and personal life, to some extent, depends on global flow. Moreover, Ray notes that everyday life is the site of reproduction of global relations in which social actors sustain globalisation through patterns of interaction and construction of social orders (Ray 2007, p. 42). The idea of globalisation causes commitment in everyday life where social interaction and social relations retain the idea of globalisation. Globalisation is an ongoing social process whereby the apparatus of globalisation is actioned by social practices. Globalisation might cause a change in the social process and, as seen in everyday life, might somehow relate to the term 'liquid modernity'.

Bauman (2007, p. 1) proposes a shift from solid to a liquid modernity that is diffuse, all-permeating and all-penetrating leading to the release of individual freedom, the process of deregulation, flexibilisation, the radical disengagement of free agents from the system, and the unlocking of individual choices (In Gane 2001, pp. 268–269).

Liquid modernity refers to a generalised impact of globalisation, and shows the interpenetration of the global into the local, which liberates social forms from structures and institutions. Bauman's theory of liquid modernity as a social condition focuses on change in individuals' everyday lives that become freed from social structures and social institutions, as a result of individuals engaging in multiple choices. Bauman's viewpoint is similar to Giddens's, with both paying attention to changes on a micro level. Individual lives and choices appear to be more fluid and flexible, and social forms can be deconstructed and reconstructed. But Giddens perceives this as an ongoing social process whereby globalisation becomes embedded in personal life, whereas Bauman sees this as a social condition that makes individual lives adapt to changes induced by global flow. Individuals are not tied to tradition and local context, and have the freedom to choose and adapt to other cultures, or recreate their own. In other words, with the disengagement of social institutions and traditions, local people are exposed to globalisation to a greater extent than before.

Some characterise globalisation as a trans-phenomenon. Bartelson (2000, p. 184) views globalisation as 'transference', which means exchange across existing unit boundaries, and between units and systems, yet this presupposes that this system, along with the units, remain the same throughout the globalising process. 'Transference' refers to the interaction between social units and is an ongoing process. Globalisation seems to be a homogenised process in which there is exchange between identical units. Globalisation can de-spatialise and de-temporalise human practices and the conditions of human knowledge, which can project onto the global as a condition of its existence (Bartelson 2000, p. 189). Human practices and human knowledge facilitate the existence of globalisation. Our consciousness of identical units and systems across space and time enables social practices and knowledge to expand. In other words, globalisation depends on how we perceive it. With exchange across units and systems, globalisation pertains to plurality rather than singularity.

According to the aforementioned theories, globalisation has a significant and generalised impact on society. As an ongoing process, it happens to reshape social forms, social practices and individuals' way of life. The influence of globalisation permeates into social units and everyday life, which change according to the global flow. However, to what extent does globalisation have a homogenised impact on society? Globalisation that refers to the complexity of social phenomena and the implosion of social dimensions may affect social forms and social practices differently.

Looking back at Giddens, he seems to treat globalisation as isolating, something that happens to change everyday life, and is dependent upon the emergence of other social events. Concerning Ray's work, patterns of social interaction and social practices reproduce the apparatus of globalisation. Although these retain the idea of globalisation and contribute to the commitment to the apparatus, they may be part of a homogenised yet fragmented process. For instance, social communication on Facebook is the outcome of global communication and fosters extended networks. Social community on Facebook may include some groups of people while excluding others, such as those who might not have access to the internet or who are prohibited from communicating with one another on Facebook due to political authorities and national regulations, for example, citizens of mainland China and North Korea. In this case, globalisation does not bring about a homogenised social process.

Regarding Bauman's liquid modernity, it is the consequence of globalisation, or, where the former is the precondition of the latter. Social forms can be deconstructed and reconstructed. But does globalisation liberalise all social forms? Some social forms may be affected by global flow, while others, such as indigenous culture and national identity, may be fixed and only slightly affected by globalisation. Globalisation is thus a homogenised but fragmented process. It has a different impact depending on the context.

In relation to 'transference', globalisation facilitates exchange between different social units, which makes human practices and human knowledge expand across space and time. These social forms support the existence of globalisation and its causes, and reproduce ideological commitment. But, again, the exchange between units and systems may be uneven, depending on the context. The generalised impact of globalisation does not only appear as a social process, but also the interaction between the global and the local.

Globalisation as the binary opposition of global and local

Globalisation may refer to the binary opposition between the West and the non-Western world. Oke (2009, p. 323) suggests that we need to understand the relationship between the West and the non-West, 'for it is the non-Western world which is the site of expansion and spread in the scale of social processes (2009, p. 323). In this case, globalisation only refers to Westernisation, and the non-West is the receptive site of the prevalent globalisation.

Globalisation constitutes the dualism of the West and the non-West. The apparatus of globalisation generates binary opposition. However, globalisation might be able to create other social forms that do not restrict this to binary opposition, particularly the relationship between the non-West and the non-West, such as the spread of Korean pop culture in Asian countries. Since globalisation permeates the local, social forms are not tied to locality, but are rather a mixture of the global and the local. Moreover, globalisation involves the adaptation of the global to the local and vice versa. Globalisation therefore constitutes the binary opposition of the global and local. The following literature discusses this issue.

Giddens introduces the conceptual framework of time-space distanciation, which involves the complex relations between local involvement (circumstances of co-presence), and interaction across distance (the connections of presence and absence) (Giddens 1990, p. 64). For Giddens, globalisation refers to the extension of social relations and social interaction between one locale and other distant locales. The consequences of local transformation do not happen in a uniform direction, but rather have divergent tendencies (Giddens 1990, p. 64). What happens in one locale can affect other distant locales and vice versa.

In terms of time-space distanciation, Giddens stresses the dimension of locality, which is the interaction between presence and absence, and yet we still cannot see how the idea of the local is developed. Giddens does not show how the local becomes constitutive in globalisation. His work offers us another version of a dualism between the global and the local. In this case, the local might not have a meaning as a single unit, for its existence relies on its involvement in global events, or it needs to be present in globalisation in order for it to exist. Moreover, there are different concepts of capturing the cultural consequence of globalisation that stress the importance of locality.

In order to stress the importance of locality, 'glocalisation' is introduced. Glocalisation is the interaction between the global and the local that maintains the dimension of locality. Robertson proposes,

> A lifted locality which refers to a sense of locality that is communicated from above has to be a standardised form of the local, and this standardisation diminishes the notion that localities are things in themselves, albeit rendering meaningful the very idea of locality.
>
> (Robertson 2012, p. 195)

For Robertson, locality is constructed from above. Although the idea of locality exists, it does not mean something in itself and is subject to the influence of globalisation. The idea of local thus accords with globalisation. Glocalisation results from the interaction between the global and the local, and seems to be a social form that incorporates the dimension of locality into the global form. However, locality is a sub-process of globalisation, or the outcome of globalisation. Therefore, what constitutes glocalisation and the idea of local is here global, and the idea of local is subject to the global extent.

In addition to Robertson, Ritzer views global as opposed to local.

Glocalisation can be coined as the interpenetration of the global and the local, which can result in unique outcomes in different geographical areas in favour of cultural heterogeneity, while grobalisation is defined as the imperialistic ambitions of nations, corporations, organisations and other entities who desire to impose themselves on various geographic areas.

(Ritzer 2003, pp. 193–194)

The binary opposition between 'grobalisation' and 'glocalisation' does not show how the local becomes constituted in globalisation, in which only affiliation to globalisation makes sense of locality. Again, the binary opposition of global and local might not add anything new to globalisation. The local has no agency. To go further than Robertson, Ritzer (2007, p. 32) believes that the idea of locality disappears and that the local is subverted by globalisation. With the interpenetration of the global into the local, the local becomes modified. The relationship between the global and the local is an imbalance.

Khondker also uses the concept of glocalisation to show a transformation of locality in globalisation, by pointing out that

glocalisation involves blending, mixing and adapting two or more processes, one of which must be local, and glocalisation needs to include at least one component that addresses the local culture, system of values and practices in order to become meaningful.

(Khondker 2004, p. 6)

For him, the glocalisation process integrates local culture into other cultures.

Khondker, (2004, p. 4), building on Robertson's framework, expresses the localisation of globality as the twin processes of macro-localisation along with micro-globalisation which the former is the expansion of local boundaries, and the making of some local ideas and practices global, whereas the latter refers to incorporating certain global processes into the local setting.

Using these two terms enables us to reposition the local upon the global stage. Although Khondker's terms reflect dimensions of locality, 'macro-localisation' as well as 'micro-globalisation' seem to be tautologies of glocalisation. Glocalisation is the adaptation of the global to the local and vice versa, which sustains the dimension of locality. Macro-localisation is implicated in glocalisation as the expansion of the local boundary in order to adapt to the global. For example, a Thai restaurant in Windermere,[1] UK, where Thai food is cooked by a local English chef, offers Thai food that suits Western tastes rather than that of Thais.

This shows how local culture is practised and experienced globally. Observed globally, local culture might be adapted and altered to suit a diverse group of people. Micro-globalisation is also similar to glocalisation, as it focuses on how global components become integrated into a locality. What is incorporated into the local might generate a new cultural form that includes local culture, such as rice with spicy fried chicken, as served in KFC restaurants in Thailand. The fried chicken is KFC's own recipe, while rice is a staple food for Thai people.

To differentiate the local from the global, Kellner proposes that 'globalisation from below bolsters an eruption of forces along with subcultures of resistance that aim to preserve specific forms of culture and society so as to create alternative forces of social and culture that fight against globalisation' (Kellner 2002, pp. 293–294). In this way, the local can resist and react to globalisation, which might affect how globalisation is constituted in a different way. Kellner seems to offer another binary opposition of globalisation, that globalisation from below is implicitly juxtaposed with globalisation from above that is regulated by the system. Globalisation from above might widen the opportunity for the local to form a group, or reinvent a subculture, through which the world can hear their story. An example of this is when people in Okinawa protested against American military presence in Japan. Local people on Okinawa demonstrated against global security led by US military bases, with the murder of a local woman and other controversial issues having encouraged them to stage a rally against the military presence (McCurry 2016). The idea of local, or globalisation from below, only emerges when the preceding global event and the right conditions take place. Without a global event, there might be no reason for the local to group together. Looking back at the example, there would not have been a local protest had there not been an American military presence in Japan. The presence of the local is dependent on the condition of global events; thus, the idea of locality is not free from the influence of global events.

Globalisation from below also implies the co-operation of multiple localities across boundaries rather than a particular local context, meaning its effect might vary within a different local context, such as the environmental movement in developed countries compared with its presence in developing countries. I doubt to what degree globalisation from below can generate the idea of the local in itself. Again, the idea of the local only becomes meaningful when it corresponds with globalisation. These theories emphasise the importance of the binary oppositions of global and local, however, is the local really an alternative to globalisation? In contrast to the concept of the binary opposition between the global and the local, Scholte contends that differentiation between the global and the local is a problem. The interrelatedness of dimensions of social space suggests that it is a mistake to set up opposition between the global and the local, and events are not global or national or local, but rather an intersection of the global and other spatial qualities (Scholte 2002, pp. 26–28). In this sense, the global seems to be the same process as the local and vice versa.

Scholte views the fact that global flows engage with people's everyday lives (listening to the radio or consuming brand-name fast foods), yet various local cultures are contrived, thus there is nothing intrinsically alienating about the global and nothing inherently liberating about the local (Scholte 2002, p. 28). The differentiation between the global and the local seems to be a problem, for globalisation inevitably affects the creation of locality. Rather, Scholte emphasises globalisation as the intersection of the global and the local, with the two overlapping. What constitutes people's everyday lives might not be either inherently global or local, since people are able to indigenise cultures, an example being Thai people using a spoon and a fork to eat pasta. They not only adapt Italian culture to the local, but also indigenise culture. Using a spoon and a fork to eat pasta is neither intrinsically Italian nor Thai, and so global and local cultures overlap.

Although globalisation is termed 'global', it does not produce a homogenised effect. The effect of globalisation varies according to the conditions as well as the context of locale. In order to critically discuss and conceptualise the effects of globalisation, I use Baudrillard's theory, which will be presented in Chapter 4. Although Baudrillard is not a globalisation theorist, his work is based on an economic-cultural approach that enables us to see how globalisation is constituted, and how it impacts upon each locale differently.

Conclusion

Globalisation seems to be an independent event that causes significant change in contemporary society, however there is no single way to capture globalisation, for it is not something that happens independently but, rather, is something that is dependent upon the emergence of other social events. Existing globalisation theories offer us insightful and critical views on globalisation, although they still treat it as a totality. Forms of globalisation may vary according to different contexts.

In some cases, globalisation is an ongoing social process that has generalised impacts on locales. It embeds in the social order, social practices and everyday life of individuals. Despite its global attribute, globalisation does not have an uneven effect on locale. The effect of globalisation is subject to the conditions of the local context, such as religious faith, political regulations and more besides. Additionally, globalisation triggers a social form, which is the binary opposition of the global and local, whereby there is a differentiation between the global and local. Still, is local an alternative to global? What appears as globalisation implies local and vice versa. In this manner, the idea of locality does not exist independently, but is created socially in conjunction with the complexity of structural forms of globalisation, and with the implosion of the global and local. Having elaborated on globalisation literature, the next chapter will discuss tourism in Thailand.

Note

1 There are many Thai restaurants in the UK, most of which are run by Thai or Asian people, while some are franchise restaurants, for example, Busaba Eathai and Chao-phraya. I was really impressed with the Jintana Thai Restaurant in Windermere, where European waitresses who dressed up in traditional Thai costume could pronounce the names of Thai food. Of course, the food was not authentic Thai, but it was great to see how Thai food was adapted to the UK context.

References

Appadurai, A. (1996). *Modernity at Large: Cultural Dimensions of Globalization.* Minneapolis: University of Minnesota Press.

Bartelson, J. (2000). Three Concepts of Globalization. *International Sociology*, 15(2), 180–196.

Bauman, Z. (2007). *Liquid Times: Living in an Age of Uncertainty*. Cambridge: Polity.

Brown, G.W. (2008). Globalization Is What We Make of It: Contemporary Globalization Theory and the Future Construction of Global Interconnection. *Political Studies Review*, 6(1), 42–53.

Castells, M. (2010). *The Rise of the Network Society*, 2nd edn. Chichester: Wiley-Blackwell.

Featherstone, M. (1995). *Undoing Culture: Globalisation, Postmodernism and Identity*. London: Sage.

Flynn, B. (2015). Superbad. *The Sun* [Online]. 2 November. Available from: www.thesun.co.uk/archives/news/119764/superbad/. [Accessed 18 April 2017].

Gane, N. (2001). Review Essay: Zygmunt Bauman: Liquid Modernity and Beyond. *ACTA Sociologica*, 44(3), 267–275.

Giddens, A. (1990). *The Consequences of Modernity*. Cambridge: Polity.

Giddens, A. (2002). *Runaway World: How Globalisation Is Reshaping Our Lives*, Rev. edn. London: Profile Books Ltd.

Hannerz, U. (2004). Cosmopolitanism. In: D. Nugent and J. Vincent (eds), *A Companion to the Anthropology of Politics*. Oxford: Blackwell Publishing Ltd, pp. 69–86.

Harvey, D. (2001). *Spaces of Capital: Towards a Critical Geography*. Edinburgh: Edinburgh University Press.

Held, D. and McGrew, A. (eds) (2000). *The Global Transformations Reader: An Introduction to the Globalization Debate*. Cambridge: Polity.

Held, D. and McGrew, A. (2002). *Globalization/Anti-Globalization*. Cambridge: Polity.

Hirst, P. and Thompson, G. (1992). The Problem of 'Globalization': International Economic Relations, National Economic Management and the Formation of Trading Blocs. *International Journal of Human Resource Management*, 21(4), 357–396.

Holton, R. (2000). Globalization's Cultural Consequences. *Annals of the American Academy of Political and Social Science*, 570(1), 140–152.

Kellner, D. (2002). Theorizing Globalization. *Sociological Theory*, 20(3), 285–305.

Khondker, H.H. (2004). Glocalization as Globalisation: Evolution of a Sociological Concept. *Bangladesh E-Journal of Sociology*, 1(2), 1–9.

Martell, L. (2007). The Third Wave in Globalization Theory. *International Studies Review*, 9(2), 1–32.

McCurry, J. (2016). Thousands Protest at US Bases on Okinawa after Japanese Woman's Murder. *The Guardian* [Online]. 19 June. Available from: www.theguardian.com/world/2016/jun/19/thousands-protest-at-us-bases-on-okinawa-after-japanese-womans. [Accessed 26 February 2017].

Oke, N. (2009). Globalizing Time and Space: Temporal and Spatial Considerations in Discourses of Globalization. *International Political Sociology*, 3, 310–326.

Rantanen, T. (2005). Giddens and the 'G'-word: An Interview with Anthony Giddens. *Global Media and Communication*, 1(1), 63–77.

Ray, L. (2007). *Globalization and Everyday Life*. Abingdon: Routledge.

Ritzer, G. (2003). Rethinking Globalization: Glocalization/Grobalization and Something/Nothing. *Sociological Theory*, 21(3), 193–209.

Ritzer, G. (2007). *The Globalization of Nothing*, 2nd edn. Thousand Oaks, CA: Pine Forge Press.

Robertson, R. (2012). Globalization or Glocalization? *The Journal of International Communication*, 18(2), 191–208.

Rosenberg, J. (2005). Globalization Theory: A Post Mortem. *International Politics*, 42(1), 2–74.

Scholte, J.A. (2002). What Is Globalisation? the Definitional Issue – Again. *CSGR Working Paper*, 109(2), 2–34.

Smith, A.D. (1990). Towards a Global Culture? *Theory, Culture and Society*, 7(2/3), 171–191.

Wang, G. and Yueh, E. (2005). Globalization and Hybridization in Cultural Products: The Cases of Mulan and Crouching Tiger, Hidden Dragon. *International Journal of Cultural Studies*, 8(2), 175–193.

3   Conceptualising tourism

Introduction

This chapter concerns tourism. Since tourism is an aspect of globalisation, what happens in globalisation parallels what happens in tourism. Similar to what happens in globalisation, the complexity of social events and the implosion of social dimensions are embedded in tourism. The effects of globalisation and tourism vary according to different local contexts. There are many ways to conceptualise tourism. This chapter first discusses the relevant literature on tourism that focuses on the dichotomies and performance in tourism, and then looks at examples of Thailand's tourism.

When the dichotomy of the home-and-away experience and tourist performance is present, a place becomes a tourist attraction. These aspects also make that place produce and reproduce cultural value in tourism. This chapter suggests that the value of local culture in tourism can be recreated in different processes of tourism. The relevant literature on floating markets and Thailand's tourism will be discussed.

The division between home-and-away experience

Tourism can be regarded as a social process that is the division of working time and free time, or that it anchors itself in the dichotomy of home and away, or leisure and work. Urry's first work on the 'tourist gaze' contends that tourism is a leisure activity, presupposing its opposite is regulated and organised work; work and leisure, therefore, appear organised as separate spheres of social practice in modern society (Urry 1990, p. 2). As a leisure activity, tourism seems to offer us free time in opposition to the regulated time that is present in the realm of work. In the second edition of *The Tourist Gaze*, he proposes that the rapid flows of tourists across national borders cause the making and re-making of places as recipients of such flows; the de-differentiation of corporeal travel from virtual travel; and the growth of tourism reflexivity that allows places to monitor, evaluate and develop their tourism potential within the emerging patterns of global tourism (Urry 2001, p. 1).

Globalisation and flows of tourism make a place enter or re-enter the tourist stage. People do not have to physically travel to a faraway place, they are able to gaze upon that place virtually. So, globalisation facilitates multiple forms of tourist gazes (Urry 2001, p. 8). The difference between the two editions of *The Tourist Gaze* is the influence of globalisation on tourist gazes. However, what remains significant in the tourist gaze is the division of the home experience and the 'other' experience. The 'other' experience has different meanings in different contexts, for example, an Oriental gaze upon a Western site and vice versa (Urry 2001, p. 2). Whether people see a site as interesting and distinctive depends on their home experience as well as their presupposition. For example, foreign tourists view floating markets in Thailand as exotic because they offer local Thai ambience, which is different from what they experience back home.

Urry and Larsen's latest work on the tourist gaze is anchored in the division between the ordinary/everyday and extraordinary. It involves daydreaming and the anticipation of new and different experiences from those normally encountered in everyday life (Urry and Larsen 2011, p. 51). Tourism is the *act* of experiencing something new and different from everyday life. The latest notion of the tourist gaze differs from Urry's first. The division between the ordinary and extraordinary may sound similar to that between working time and free time, yet they are not the same. What we encounter in everyday life includes working time and can extend beyond working time, such as local culture, tradition, lifestyle, idea, daily life and so on. In this case, tourism can emancipate people from the regulation of work. When people travel to a new place, they are able to do things they are not able to do in everyday life. Tourism allows people to enjoy their time and have freedom.

Extraordinary experience may be associated with 'otherness'. The emphasis placed on gazing upon 'the other' marks Urry's work as postmodern tourism (see further, Uriely 1997, p. 983). Regarding 'the other' in postmodern tourism, Munt (1994, pp. 102–112) notes that postmodern tourism pertains to 'otherness' characterised by the growth of interest in non-Western cultures, religious traditions, ethnicity, environment and ecology in Third and Fourth World countries. Non-Western cultures in less developed countries become the objects of the tourist gaze. A place becomes a tourist attraction on the condition that it maintains its aura of 'otherness'. Of floating markets in Thailand, Cohen (2016, p. 67) says the recreation of them serves to promote an image of nostalgia, including that felt by middle-class Thais who yearn for a romanticised, quieter and simpler way of life similar to that seen in the period before Bangkok was expanded and modernised, especially with regard to the old riverside culture and houses of waterside markets. Visiting floating markets enables Thai and foreign tourists to gaze upon 'the other'. The markets remind Thai tourists of old Thai culture, while foreign tourists see an outmoded way of life. Floating markets are different from what they experience in their everyday lives. In this way, 'otherness' is associated with extraordinary experience.

However, MacCannell argues that Urry's tourist gaze posits the tourist as a kind of subject who does not experience something extraordinary at home and therefore does not have 'interest value' in his daily life (MacCannell 2001, p. 25). MacCannell does not see tourism as an extraordinary experience, for people can encounter extraordinary things at home. What we face in our daily lives may include both the usual things and the extraordinary. In addition, we may ask what extent of 'otherness' do tourists expect to see? People might not want to experience something that is too extraordinary, or completely 'other', but rather, something in between. According to Ritzer and Liska (1997, p. 101), 'For many of those who desire to see the extraordinary, there is also a desire to have McDonaldized stops (standardised experiences) along the way, and to retreat to non-McDonaldized and McDonaldized elements'. To some extent, it might be true that tourist attractions juxtapose with a McDonaldized (standardised and homogenised) experience, and a non-McDonaldized or diversified experience.

Tourists might want to have something that is similar to their everyday life, while expecting to see some differences. For instance, they might prefer travelling to floating markets outside Bangkok as part of a group tour, rather than travelling independently. Not only might this be a more comfortable way to travel, and it might be convenient, but they might also want to stick together. Sometimes they want to have an ordinary experience with other foreign tourists so that they can feel more at ease and not experience a complete culture shock.

As Haldrup and Larsen say, 'Tourists never just travel *to* places: their mindsets, routines and social relations travel *with* them, thereby the imaginative geographies of tourism are as much about "home" as faraway places' (2010, p. 27). With this presupposition and the backgrounds of tourists, tourism engages the interplay between home and away experience. Haldrup and Larsen suggest that unlike the sign-consumption of the tourist gaze, material objects remain crucial in tourism.

> Leisure and tourism practices are much more tied up with material objects and physical sensations than traditionally assumed, and emblematic tourist performances involve, and are made possible and pleasurable by, objects, machines and technologies.
>
> (Haldrup and Larsen 2006, p. 275)

Tourist performance is a combination of materiality and the senses. Tourist practices depend on the material culture of a place, and tourists perform in accordance with objects and physical sensations of the place. 'Tourist things can acquire use value through being employed in embodied practices, in and through the sensuous materiality of the body' (Haldrup and Larsen 2006, p. 278). Use-value of tourist objects depends on how we sense the object, and thus it is subjective. Apart from the home and away experience, does tourism have other implications?

Authenticity and cultural value

Apart from 'otherness', what tourists gaze upon more or less relates to authenticity.

Walter Benjamin emphasises that authenticity is connected with aura, since they both result from and are embedded in ritual and tradition, in that authenticity of the object/site is a result of its embodiment in a tradition of which tourism is a ritual. The authenticity of the experience is a part of an engagement with aura (Benjamin cited in Rickly-Boyd 2012, p. 271). Thus, the value of authenticity is linked with aura, and authenticity relates to tradition and ritual. In order to obtain an authentic experience, people need to be immersed in aura. Authenticity does not inherently occur in an object or place, it is socially constructed.

Furthermore, Wang differentiates types of authenticity: *objective authenticity* refers to a museum-linked usage of the authenticity of the original that is also the object to be perceived by tourists. *Constructive authenticity* is something that may appear to be authentic because it is constructed in terms of points of view, belief and from the perspective of power (Wang 1999, p. 351). When visiting a tourist place, tourists can delve into authenticity that adheres both to objects and experiences. Authenticity appears to be subjective and is based upon the perception and interpretation of individuals. Authenticity is socially created in objects and activities. Looking at Wang's work, it is not clear how objective authenticity works in tourism. Although she links objective authenticity to the museum-tourism context, objects viewed in a museum might be constructive and subjective, depending on how tourists perceive and interpret them. Benjamin and Wang view authenticity differently, yet they share one view in common: authenticity is constructed socially in tourism, depending upon the interaction between the global and the local.

In contrast, MacCannell thinks the quest for authenticity is the quest for real culture. He proposes the desire for authentic experiences makes tourists enter the settings front and backstage, which are arranged in a continuum starting at the front and ending at the back (MacCannell 2013, p. 101). The front stage is openly set up for tourists, while the back stage is more or less composed of authentic and real culture. The problem is that tourists always end up in settings decorated to resemble the back stage, or even a false back, which present only copies of real culture that reveal more realness than the culture itself (MacCannell 2013, p. 102). MacCannell believes tourists search for authentic and real culture, and it seems that they may simultaneously encounter the front and back stage in one tourist location. Or rather, what they see as authentic culture may merely be staged. If a place offers real authentic culture, will it be enough to attract tourists to visit that place?

Authenticity might not be the top priority of the tourist experience. As Boorstin (1962, p. 114) contends, 'The tourist rarely likes the authentic product of the foreign culture, he prefers his own provincial expectations'. In this case, authenticity may not be the most important goal for tourists, rather, they expect to see spurious objects and places. Contrived culture and spurious objects may look attractive to tourists and they may be impressed with a contrived culture that is well presented in a place, rather than searching for the real culture itself. Authenticity is thus all about producing cultural value and cultural content of the place/object.

Inevitably, the production of cultural value and cultural content seems to involve globalisation. Ritzer reduces the global phenomenon to the dichotomy of 'something' and 'nothing': 'Nothing means a social form that is generally centrally conceived, controlled and is comparatively devoid of distinctive substantive content, while something is a social form that is generally indigenously conceived, controlled and comparatively rich in distinctive substantive content' (Ritzer 2003, p. 195). The concept of 'something-nothing' implicitly refers to the cultural content of an object and a place. 'Something' means distinctive local cultural content, whereas 'nothing' is the generic cultural form.

Ritzer uses the continuum of 'something and nothing' with that of 'grobalisation and glocalisation' (please see the previous chapter for further detail). The differentiation of something from nothing fosters what Ritzer calls 'an elective affinity, whereby grobalisation (nothing) and glocalisation (something) mutually incline to combine with one another' (Ritzer 2007, p. 121). For him, one of the best examples of the glocalisation of nothing is to be found in tourism, such as in souvenirs, local performances and local meals (Ritzer 2007, pp. 130–131).

What involves globalisation and tourism is devoid of unique cultural content. It might be true that most tourist places are filled with indistinctive cultural content. For example, Damnoen Saduak Floating Market waters down its local cultural content, as it does not appear to be a fruit market anymore. As already discussed, since the advent of road transportation and the arrival of tourists, what is being sold, is tourist orientated. However, this seems to be a normal process of globalisation, with the global meeting the local, whereby such a locale, in this case, floating markets and local people, must adapt themselves to globalisation in order for their culture to continue to exist. Apart from authenticity and cultural value, what else can produce and reproduce a tourist place?

Tourism as performance: tourist performance or performance of local people

In this section, literature on tourism that focuses on performance in tourism is discussed. In contrast to Urry's tourist gaze, MacCannell proposes a second gaze in favour of tourist agency and consumption. He says the human subject, or tourist, can perform the second gaze, whereby they know there is always something hidden from the foreground, and the gaze is a work in progress combining the way to re-read and interpret what is presented at a tourist site (MacCannell 2001, p. 36). Tourists are able to exercise agency in gazing upon each object and site, or not gaze at all. They may not follow the script of the holiday place.

Tourist performance is not merely about tourist agency but also informs everydayness and routine. Larsen notes that we should redirect our attention to a 'performance turn' in which tourism is embedded with everyday practices, ordinary places and significant others, such as meeting someone at a distance, meaning tourists always travel to places with their own mindsets, routines and social relations (Larsen 2008, pp. 26–27). Tourism extends social relations in everyday life and people can acquire a sense of place from being with a significant other in a different place.

Also, Edensor (2001, p. 60) sees tourism as a process involving the ongoing reconstruction of a space in a shared context, as this is not determined by the prevalence of codes and norms, since tourist conventions can be deconstructed by rebellious performances, as well as by multiple simultaneous actions on the same stage. For Edensor, tourist performance varies according to the context. Although codes and norms of tourist practice exist, tourists do not have to follow the script. They can interpret norms and codes of practice differently. Tourist performance can be resistant and improvised. There is no separation of the everyday from tourism, for these two overlap. On the one hand, tourist performance is conditioned by the everyday, ordinary or home experience, whereas on the other, the norms and codes of holidays and tourist places affect their performance. Thus, tourist performance is something in between.

Additionally, Sheller and Urry present 'the playfulness of place', in other words,

> the ways in which places themselves are always 'on the move'. Places are 'performed', often on a kind of global stage, and in these performances they are put into play in relation to other places becoming more or less desirable, more or less visited.
>
> (Sheller and Urry 2004, p. 1)

Flows of tourism may cause the emergence/re-emergence of the place, or even the disappearance of the place. We can take Thailand as an example. Thailand, as the destination country, attracts different groups of tourists. According to Kontogeorgopoulos,

> Traditionally, travellers from the US and Western Europe (Britain and France in particular) made up the majority of tourist arrivals in Thailand, yet from the mid-1970s onwards, tourists from Japan and other countries in Asia, including South Korea, Hong Kong, Singapore and Taiwan, came to form the dominant group of tourists in Thailand.
>
> (Kontogeorgopoulos 1998, p. 228)

Western tourists and Asian tourists may have different expectations. Additionally, the latter are generally little concerned with authenticity (Cohen and Cohen, in Cohen 2016, p. 69). Between 1990 and 1995, Thailand became the destination for Chinese tourists who principally wanted to visit their relatives and friends after the Mainland Chinese government added Thailand to the list of Approved Destination Status countries, which included Singapore, Malaysia, Russia, Mongolia and the Philippines (Guo, Kim, and Timothy 2007, p. 314). The arrival of Chinese tourists facilitated by political factors and the growth of the Chinese economy reshaped tourist sites in Thailand to meet their expectations, which Pattaya Floating Market does.

Different places are interconnected with one another on the tourist stage. For example, different floating markets in Thailand attract different groups of tourists. The revival of Damnoen Saduak Floating Market, the best-known floating market internationally, targeted foreign tourists and has seen a rise in Asian tourists visiting the site in recent years, while Amphawa, Sam Chuk and Taling Chan Floating Markets are among the most popular sightseeing and culinary places for Thai weekend excursionists (Cohen 2016, pp. 67 and 69). However, the main target group for Pattaya Floating Market is tourists who visit Pattaya city, particularly Asian and Chinese tourists (Pongajarn, Van der Duim, and Peters 2016, p. 10). Domestic and international tourism has caused different floating markets to become tourist attractions.

Not only does tourist performance reproduce a place but also the performance of local people. Some theorists view that tourism causes disadvantage to local people. For instance, Azarya (2004, p. 965) asserts that 'the economic incorporation opportunities are dependent on a continued representation of cultural marginality, as an ultimate paradox of globalisation'. Although natives do stand to gain economically from certain touristic encounters, they can only do so by performing a set of traditions derived largely from the Western imagination (Silver 1993, p. 310). Economic benefits from tourism paradoxically represent the cultural marginality of local people. With tourism, the cultural performance of local people is framed by Western expectations and imaginations. Local people become subordinated to the flows of tourism.

> MacCannell also viewed the form of ingesting the other into the self and then eliminating it as contemporary cannibalism, where tourists consume and destroy local culture in developing countries.
>
> (in Wearing and Wearing 2001, p. 152)

Tourism, thus, results in cultural marginalisation and even the absence of local culture. The arrival of tourists waters down and destroys local culture. Culture, along with the identity of local people, is affected by tourism flows; in this way, local people are deprived of agency. However, tourism may not necessarily water down local culture. Rather, it could widen opportunities for local people to reinvent it in order to adapt to tourism flows. With the construction of a local culture, some theorists argue that there is agency of local people in tourism. Judd emphasises that the tourist experience is manufactured by institutions and actors, it is then priced within a market system, and the tourist experience receives the highest value-added inputs to the commodity chain of tourism, flow from design, marketing and information technology management (Judd 2006, p. 328).

Tourism does not spontaneously occur, yet it is an ongoing process of production. Local people are able to exercise agency so as to construct culture and add value to a place. Instead of being disadvantaged by tourism, local people are a productive force in manufacturing tourist objects and tourist places, where they can play an important role in marketing, managing information technology and advertising. The interaction between the global and local brings about the production of cultural meaning.

Gotham sees tourism as an uneven and contested process involving a set of global forces imposed from above, in conjunction with localised actions and organisations that attempt to preserve place difference and local traditions; therefore, local people can get involved in the production of meaning (Gotham 2005, pp. 311, 322).

Tourism is not externally imposed on by the global, rather it is simultaneously mediated by the local people as they can reinvent the cultural meaning of a place. In this way, tourism seems to involve both globalised and localised processes. Global flows adapt to the local and vice versa. Local people can produce cultural meaning while preserving local culture at the same time. Wood speaks of tourism that is appropriated by local people and used to symbolically construct culture, tradition and identity; globalisation always gets mediated by local factors so as to produce unique outcomes in different locations (cited in Teo and Li 2003, p. 288). Globalisation of tourism does happen locally and results in different outcomes in different places because local people are able to mediate globalisation and reinvent local culture through the manipulation of cultural signs including symbols, ideas and meaning.

In stressing the importance of local people in production, Dicks (2003, pp. 1, 17, 61 and 65) says culture, central to the production of visibility, makes a place become somewhere to go, local people can then re-appropriate some of the surplus value for themselves by engaging as vendors of tourist services, and in self-display, as if for an audience.

The production of culture makes a place become a tourist attraction, and this marks a place as viewable on the tourist stage. As producers, local people are able to benefit from tourism when they sell tourist objects, offer tourist experiences and involve themselves in manipulating local culture for tourists. In this manner, local people are able to exercise agency in producing and retaining local culture. Due to the agency of local actors, a productive workforce and production processes are important. Local people are productive in creating tourism objects and places, and they include in them the production of meaning and cultural value.

There may well be no tourist experience without the producer and the production process. Looking at floating markets in Thailand, the revival of Amphawa Floating Market in Samut Songkhram Province is based on production and local-people performance. According to Vajirakachon and Nepal (2014, p. 8), Amphawa Floating Market, known for its community-based tourism product, became Thailand's primary tourist attraction, and local residents regarded this as improving their livelihood opportunities after the mayor had revived the floating market in 2004. In this case, local people played an important role in recreating the value of the floating market in Thailand's tourism.

Rather than juxtaposing tourism with the consumption-production axis, Milne and Ateljevic (2001, p. 386) state that tourism is a phenomenon that comprises a collage of producing and consuming moments, which is essentially a global process, manifesting itself locally and regionally, and explicitly causing the construction of a place. Tourism is dependent on the interplays between production and consumption, and between the global and the local. These can recreate value in local culture.

In addition to the discussions above, tourism is inevitably associated with globalisation. The following section will look at this.

Globalisation and tourism

The existing literature discusses the interrelatedness of globalisation and tourism, and the following examples expand on this. Reiser (2003, p. 310) proposes that globalisation and tourism are connected in many different ways, in particular, the movement of people, ideas and capital across borders. Globalisation and tourism share common ground with each other in these domains. Tourism becomes global, for it is involved in flows of people, flows of images and flows of capital. Some use the term 'global tourism' to highlight the interrelatedness of globalisation and tourism.

Smith (2004, p. 25) views global tourism as visitor flows, advertising, flows of spending by visitors and tourism enterprises, with tourism having become a truly global phenomenon in the 1950s because of the development of commercially viable jet aircraft capable of trans-oceanic flights. In this way, technological development in transportation is the main cause of global tourism. For Urry (2001, p. 3), global tourism makes people and places get caught up with each other, with the 'global' and 'tourism' being part of the same set of complex processes in which infrastructures, flows of images and people, along with the emerging practices of tourist reflexivity, can be captured as a 'global hybrid' that makes global tourism expand and reproduce itself across the globe. These processes enable tourists to connect with different places. They can travel to different places corporeally and virtually, and experience 'other' cultures. Each place adapts itself to flows of tourism and connects with other places.

Tourists can pass over their cultures into other places, while a local place can display local culture before tourists. Hence, Urry suggests that 'culture becomes so mobile', meaning tourists, objects, cultures and images may travel (2001, p. 6). Therefore, global tourism pertains to flows of culture across nations. In some cases, tourists do not have to travel to a faraway place, but they can expose themselves to 'other' cultures via the media and the internet. Tourism cannot be separated from the global, although tourism itself is not entirely global. Meethan contends that,

> what marks tourism as a distinct area of activity is that it is, on the one hand, the most globalised of social activities, while on the other hand, it is bound to the specificity of locales, and both globalised and localised elements are related through the cycle of production and consumption of commodities, services and places.
>
> (Meethan 2004, p. 118)

Due to flows of tourists, and of capital and of culture, tourism becomes global, yet it is a localised process in which a local place recreates culture and produces local products to be sold to tourists.

In the same vein, Chang and Huang (2004, p. 223) argue that tourism becomes global, for it entails the movement of people and of capital on a transnational scale, but simultaneously it is rooted in the local as tourists are attracted to visit different places and see distinctive cultures. Tourism is inherently local, whereby a local place becomes connected to global flows, and these trigger changes in the place of destination. With the consumption–production axis, tourism retains its global and local elements. These works enable us to understand globalisation and tourism, yet they pay attention to their interrelatedness in terms of scale of tourism. The scale of tourism is expanded as it changes from the local to the global. However, the term 'global tourism' may not indicate the effect of globalisation on tourism clearly. To define its effect, I would introduce the term 'globalised tourism'. This will be further discussed in the chapter on Baudrillard.

Conclusion

We can see that there are many ways a place may become a tourist attraction. Tourism may offer tourists a new and differentiated experience from their everyday life at home, or their social relations in everyday life may extend to tourism, for instance, people travel to a faraway place to meet a significant other. Tourism may anchor itself in a sign whereby a tourist place becomes the object of the tourist gaze. Additionally, the production of cultural value in a local tourist site involves processes of consumption and production. Tourist performance also reproduces a place. Tourists may follow the norms and codes of holidays, or their performance may be improvised depending on their presupposition. Local people also play an important role in recreating a tourist place and producing cultural value. Tourism is thus a globalised process on the one hand by which flows of capital and of tourists cause local culture to modify itself, and, simultaneously, on the other hand, tourism is a localised process by which local people can adapt themselves to flows of tourism. Tourism is a part of globalisation, and the effect of globalisation and tourism may vary according to local context.

The next chapter will move on to a specific theoretical theme of the book and introduce Baudrillard's theory.

References

Azarya, V. (2004). Globalization and International Tourism in Developing Countries: Marginality as a Commercial Commodity. *Current Sociology*, 52(6), 949–967.

Boorstin, D.J. (1962). *The Image, or What Happened to the American Dream*. Harmondsworth: Penguin Books.

Chang, T.C. and Huang, S. (2004). Urban Tourism: Between the Global and the Local. In: A.A. Lew, M. Hall and A.M. Williams (eds), *A Companion to Tourism*. Oxford: Blackwell Publishing Ltd, pp. 223–234.

Cohen, E. (2016). The Permutations of Thailand's 'Floating Markets'. *Asian Journal of Tourism Research*, 1(1), 59–98.

Dicks, B. (2003). *Culture on Display: The Production of Contemporary Visitability.* Maidenhead: Open University Press.

Edensor, T. (2001). Performing Tourism, Staging Tourism: (Re)producing Tourist Space and Practice. *Tourist Studies*, 1(1), 59–81.

Gotham, K.F. (2005). Tourism from above and Below: Globalization, Localization and New Orleans's Mardi Gras. *International Journal of Urban and Regional Research*, 29(2), 309–326.

Guo, Y., Kim, S.S. and Timothy, D. (2007). Development Characteristics and Implications of Mainland Chinese Outbound Tourism. *Asia Pacific Journal of Tourism Research*, 12(4), 313–332.

Haldrup, M. and Larsen, J. (2006). Material Cultures of Tourism. *Leisure Studies*, 25(3), 275–289.

Haldrup, M. and Larsen, J. (2010). *Tourism, Performance and the Everyday: Consuming the Orient.* Abingdon: Routledge.

Judd, D.R. (2006). Commentary: Tracing the Commodity Chain of Global Tourism. *Tourism Geographies*, 8(4), 323–336.

Kontogeorgopoulos, N. (1998). Tourism in Thailand: Patterns, Trends and Limitations. *Pacific Tourism Review*, 2(3/4), 225–238.

Larsen, J. (2008). De-Exoticizing Tourist Travel: Everyday Life and Sociality on the Move. *Leisure Studies*, 27(1), 21–34.

MacCannell, D. (2001). Tourist Agency. *Tourist Studies*, 1(1), 23–37.

MacCannell, D. (2013). *The Tourist: A New Theory of the Leisure Class.* Berkeley: University of California Press.

Meethan, K. (2004). Transnational Corporations, Globalization, and Tourism. In: A.A. Lew, M. Hall and A.M. Williams (eds), *A Companion to Tourism.* Oxford: Blackwell Publishing, pp. 110–121.

Milne, S. and Ateljevic, I. (2001). Tourism, Economic Development and the Global-Local Nexus: Theory Embracing Complexity. *Tourism Geographies*, 3(4), 369–393.

Munt, I. (1994). The 'Other' Postmodern Tourism: Culture, Travel and the New Middle Classes. *Theory, Culture & Society*, 11(3), 101–123.

Pongajarn, C., Van der Duim, R. and Peters, K. (2016). Floating Markets in Thailand: Same, Same, but Different. *Journal of Tourism and Cultural Change*, 16(2), 109–122.

Reiser, D. (2003). Globalisation: An Old Phenomenon that Needs to Be Rediscovered for Tourism. *Tourism and Hospitality Research*, 4(4), 306–320.

Rickly-Boyd, J.M. (2012). Authenticity and Aura: A Benjaminian Approach to Tourism. *Annals of Tourism Research*, 39(1), 269–289.

Ritzer, G. (2003). Rethinking Globalization: Glocalization/Grobalization and Something/ Nothing. *Sociological Theory*, 21(3), 193–209.

Ritzer, G. (2007). *The Globalization of Nothing 2.* Thousand Oaks: Pine Forge Press.

Ritzer, G. and Liska, A. (1997). McDisneyization and Post-Tourism: Complementary Perspectives on Contemporary Tourism. In: C. Rojek and J. Urry (eds), *Touring Cultures: Transformations of Travel and Theory.* Abingdon: Routledge, pp. 96–109.

Sheller, M. and Urry, J. (2004). *Tourism Mobilities: Places to Play, Places in Play.* London: Routledge.

Silver, I. (1993). Marketing Authenticity in the Third World Countries. *Annals of Tourism Research*, 20(2), 302–318.

Smith, S. (2004). The Measurement of Global Tourism: Old Debates, New Consensus, and Continuing Challenges. In: A.A. Lew, M. Hall and A.M. Williams (eds), *A Companion to Tourism.* Oxford: Blackwell Publishing, pp. 25–35.

Teo, P. and Li, H. (2003). Global and Local Interactions in Tourism. *Annals of Tourism Research*, 30(2), 287–306.

Uriely, N. (1997). Theories of Modern and Postmodern Tourism. *Annals of Tourism Research*, 24(4), 982–984.

Urry, J. (1990). *The Tourist Gaze: Leisure and Travel in Contemporary Societies*. London: Sage.

Urry, J. (2001). *Globalising the Tourist Gaze*. [Online]. Available from: www.lancaster.ac.uk/fass/resources/sociology-online-papers/papers/urry-globalising-the-tourist-gaze.pdf. [Accessed 29 August 2017].

Urry, J. and Larsen, J. (2011). *The Tourist Gaze 3.0*. London: Sage.

Vajirakachon, T. and Nepal, S. (2014). Local Perspectives of Community-Based Tourism: Case Study from Thailand's Amphawa Floating Market. *Int.J. Tourism Anthropology*, 3(4), 342–356.

Wang, N. (1999). Rethinking Authenticity in Tourism Experience. *Annals of Tourism Research*, 26(2), 349–370.

Wearing, S. and Wearing, B. (2001). Conceptualizing the Selves of Tourism. *Leisure Studies*, 20(2), 143–159.

4 Baudrillard, globalisation and tourism

Introduction

Having presented literature on globalisation and tourism, this chapter will look at Baudrillard's theory. My arguments are developed specifically in the context of that theory. This chapter introduces and explains Baudrillard's concepts, which will be used throughout the book. His ideas will be discussed as stages of representation, including signs, the play of differences, and simulacra. First, however, I approach the literature on globalisation and tourism using Baudrillard's conceptions.

Baudrillard and his contribution to the knowledge of globalisation

This book employs Baudrillard's theory in the study of globalisation. While Baudrillard is not a theorist on globalisation, I would suggest his theory can be used as an alternative way to conceptualise globalisation. It is a way of thinking 'outside the box', as there is no single way to capture globalisation. Looking back at the literature review on globalisation, there are many different opinions, but one thing the authors have in common is that they treat globalisation as a totality. Globalisation seems to be an independent social phenomenon.

However, I question to what extent globalisation exists independently. I suggest that the apparatus of globalisation is the simulation of other social events. It is constituted differently, depending on other social events. Globalisation refers to the complexity of social events and the implosion of social dimensions. To elaborate on this issue, Baudrillard's orders of simulacra will be extensively employed to critically approach globalisation. His concept enables me to think outside the box and tell the old story of globalisation in a new way.

Globalisation as a one-size-fits-all approach

Baudrillard's theory of orders of simulacra is an economic-cultural approach that is premised upon the implosion of the economy and culture, rather than on economic or cultural reductionism. Globalisation does not cause changes in social dimensions, as many globalisation theorists propose, rather, the implosion of social dimensions creates the idea of globalisation. Globalisation pertains to a multidimensional and complicated social process, thus we cannot separate one dimension from the other.

The implosion of the economy and culture facilitates a change in the law of value, which parallels each order of simulacrum. This can be used to explain how the idea of globalisation develops and reproduces itself in contemporary society. Baudrillard presents a change in the law of value in each order of simulacrum as follows:

> Three orders of appearance are parallel to the mutations of the law of value. The first order of simulacrum, governed by the natural law of value, saw the end of the obliged sign, and started welcoming the emancipated sign, through which we could transfer value or sign from one class to another and pass into counterfeit.
>
> (Baudrillard 1983, pp. 83–85)

In the first order of simulacrum, signs show the natural value of an original: where signs proliferate, those that used to be limited to class and the realm of tradition become arbitrary. In the first order of simulacrum, the counterfeit still represents an original, or rather, sign is the representation of originality.

> The second order of simulacrum, embedded in the commercial law of value, occurred during the industrial revolution and saw a new generation of signs that can be produced all at once on a gigantic scale.
>
> (Baudrillard 1983, pp. 83–96)

The second stage of simulacrum marked out by the commercial law of value refers to the capitalist economic system. The diktats of the market cause a liquidation of the sign, which does not restrict it to its initial form. A sign can be reproduced and mass-produced. The transition from the first order of simulacrum to the second order can explain a significant change in society, where social form, value and signs do not necessarily tie up with the realms of tradition and original culture. The sign becomes proliferated and exchangeable.

In connection with globalisation, those orders do not show the chronological stages of globalisation, instead each one shows how the idea of globalisation is developed, reproduced and exchanged; there is no fixed definition of globalisation. Each stage of globalisation may happen simultaneously. The apparatus of globalisation can be categorised into the following orders of simulacra: the first order is that globalisation represents other systems, such as the capitalist economy. Baudrillard suggests that, 'What is globalised is first and foremost the market, the profusion of exchanges and all sorts of products, the perpetual flow of money' (Baudrillard 2003, p. 1).

In the first stage of simulacrum, globalisation is associated with the economic system. Globalisation appears to be the representation, or the counterfeit, of the economic system, where the form of globalisation bears a resemblance to the system. Globalisation then enters the second order of simulacrum, whereby the apparatus of globalisation is mass-produced and reproduced as a series in which it becomes equivalent to single and multiple causes.

The apparatus of globalisation does not restrict it to the capitalist economic system or its original form. Rather, the idea of globalisation is exchangeable with causal factors through which it is equivalent to the global economy, global politics, global culture and technological development. Or rather, the apparatus of globalisation is constituted by the emergence of other social events. It can be drawn out from different causal factors and so does not exist independently.

The homogenised effects of globalisation

Instead of a homogenised social process, globalisation seems to be a paradox, whereby it is homogenised but simultaneously fragmented. This depends on the conditions of the social context when the apparatus of globalisation is applied. Or rather, the effect of globalisation varies according to the local context. To better capture the paradoxical attribute of globalisation, we can look back at Baudrillard's orders of simulacra. As previously noted in the literature review chapter, globalisation is a social process that permeates the way of life of individuals and reshapes social units. This may refer to the third order of simulacrum. Baudrillard emphasises that, 'We are now in the third order of simulacrum, the structural law of value, where only affiliation to the model has any meaning; hence everything proceeds from the model, the "signifier of reference"' (Baudrillard 1983, pp. 83 and 101).

In the third order of simulacrum, only the model produces social forms and structures relations between things. It does not represent and mass-produce its origin, as it does in the first and second order of simulacra, respectively. In the third stage, globalisation that once represented the economic system turns out to be an independent phenomenon that happens to structure other parts of society and everyday life. Or rather, globalisation appears to be a model that generates social process and social form. Globalisation itself can be used to explain other social events. It forgets its original form – the capitalist system – and its roots in different causal factors. Social process produced by globalisation does not have a specific end, for it is homogenised, yet simultaneously fragmented.

Martinelli (2003, p. 95) introduces globalisation as a multifaceted process with far-reaching consequences that may impose constraints yet open up opportunities for individual and collective action. Some groups of people may benefit from global flow to a higher degree than others. The effect of globalisation varies in social conditions, and the far-reaching consequences for people's lives correspond with global flow and local context. For instance, virtual communities on the internet come from a homogenised process in which people from different parts of the world are exposed to global culture and cosmopolitanism. Paradoxically, the internet enables people to reconstruct sub-cultures and indigenous cultures. Global communication does not bring about homogenisation because of fragmentation. Value and cultural meanings are exchangeable with sign and reference.

Globalisation as the binary opposition of the global and the local

Additionally, Baudrillard argues there might be no single contributor to globalisation. 'Baudrillard states globalisation has no single creator and its real locus is the world; not even America can claim to be the creator of globalisation' (Sassatelli 2002, p. 521). This implies globalisation cannot be reduced to either Westernisation or Americanisation. Globalisation may not necessarily be a Western phenomenon, but its effect varies according to the locale. Globalisation is differently constituted. As presented in Chapter 2, capturing a generalised impact of globalisation as the binary opposition of the global and the local does not add something new to globalisation and does not make globalisation happen independently. Baudrillard's theory may enable us to perceive this differently. According to him, the third order simulacrum, characterised by the structural law of value, generates a binary opposition (Baudrillard 1983, p. 103). Globalisation itself turns out to be a model or an independent social phenomenon that causes the binary opposition of the global and the local to emerge.

Although the binary opposition of the global and the local proceeds from the model of globalisation, it is not a homogenised impact of globalisation. As previously discussed, globalisation seems to be homogenised, yet paradoxically fragmented (Baudrillard 2003, p. 2). The binary opposition of the global and the local does not homogenise all social forms, but it may not bring about differentiated locality either. The effect of integration of the global and local may vary according to each context. When encountering globalisation, on the one hand, the idea of locality accords with the global, while on the other hand, local people indigenise global flow. The interaction between the global and the local constitutes different social forms in each context, which allows globalisation to permeate everyday life and social practice, reinforcing the spread of globalisation.

Additionally, what happens in globalisation is not only the interaction between the global and the local but also the implosion of the global and the local. There is no local that exists without the influence of globalisation, albeit one with an uneven impact. The idea of the local, to some extent, accords with the global, while the influence of the global cannot be realised without a local context. In this way, the boundary of the global and the local gets blurred, or they implode on each other. The idea of locality may not be an alternative to, or opposed to, globalisation, because to some extent, the existence of the local is conditioned by globalisation.

Besides, what is termed 'global' is not opposed to the local. Baudrillard calls this 'a reversal of origin and finality in the third order of simulacrum in which social forms can be diffracted from the model' (Baudrillard 1983, p. 100). The idea of locality loses its finality. It becomes open to combinatory systems of sign and reference. Rather than differentiation and singularity, the apparatus of locality can be deconstructed and reconstructed in globalisation. It becomes exchangeable with other signs and reference. The apparatus of the global does not have a specific end but depends on the context it is applied to. It is thus likely that only simulation of the local exists in globalisation, while simulation of the global only appears when it meets with the local.

Baudrillard and his contribution to contemporary tourism

Baudrillard discusses tourism and leisure in *The Consumer Society*. His perspectives on tourism and leisure are more or less influenced by Marxism. He views tourism and leisure as constrained time that causes the production of value. If tourism relates to the economic system, is tourism really any different from ordinary working time? By contrast with the chapter that covers the literature on tourism, I will suggest ordinary working time and tourism are not different from each other, for they accord with the framework of the economic system. Both ordinary working time and free time are exchangeable with money. They are bought and sold in the market. People have to spend money when they travel somewhere or engage in a leisure activity.

With the consumption-production axis, tourism involves both globalised and localised processes, and reflects the implosion of economy and culture. What is produced to be sold in a tourist market has cultural meaning and value. Value and meanings of tourist commodities are exchangeable with money. Baudrillard proposes that 'time is a rare and precious commodity that is subject to the laws of exchange-value, where working time is bought and sold, and free time needs to be directly and indirectly purchased in order for it to be consumed' (Baudrillard 1998, p. 153).

For Baudrillard, the division between working time and free time is a false division, for free time is subject to the same regulations as working time. People think that holiday time is free time, yet it is not free. They must pay for it in order to spend leisure time doing something else or travelling to another place. Capital feeds on free time just as it does on working time. Due to the law of exchange-value, free time can be reproduced and maintained. In addition, free time consumed by leisure and tourism simultaneously is a productive force of constrained time. Rather than a home-and-away experience, free time in leisure and tourism bolsters the production of value. Baudrillard highlights that free time is the freedom to waste one's time and, in this manner, it shows consumed free time is in fact the time of a production of value – distinctive value, status value and prestige value (Baudrillard 1998, pp. 154–157).

In this way, wasting one's time in leisure and tourism is, in turn, a production of value. Free time is doing something that is economically unproductive, but paradoxically a productive force of maintaining and reproducing value, namely the status value of holidaymakers. In the case of Thailand's tourism, a production of value refers to the cultural value of the destination country. Tourist arrivals enable the country to recreate and repackage Thai culture.

Although tourist performance and local people's performance can recreate tourist space, their performances are subject to the norms of holidays and the diktats of the market, respectively. In this case, their performances refer to 'constrained labour'. Tourism appears to be freedom, but paradoxically, is a constraint. Tourism and leisure do not fulfil one's own needs, but rather they reproduce the system and its norms, particularly the quest for distinctive value.

Tourists are subject to the mental and practical constraints of productive time during their holidays. Regarding tourists, Baudrillard says,

We find in leisure and holidays the same eager moral and idealistic pursuit of accomplishment as in the sphere of work, and the same ethics of pressured performance. For example, the obsession with getting a tan, that bewildered whirl in which tourists 'do' Italy, Spain, all the art galleries and the smiles all attest to the fact that tourists conform in every detail to the principles of duty, sacrifice and asceticism.

(Baudrillard 1998, pp. 155–156)

In the realm of leisure and tourism, tourists are subject to a constrained performance just as they are in the realm of work. People might think that tourism and leisure help them break the cycle of work, but actually, they are not released from the system, their time is not, in fact, free. For Baudrillard, rather than being performers and consumers, tourists instead become labour and the productive force of time. Pressurised tourist performance varies with different locales, or destination countries, for example, sun, sea and sand are tourist expectations when taking holidays in Thailand.

Apart from tourists, another group of labour is local people, or producers, who, in turn, sacrifice their free time to work for tourists, producing objects for sale. Thus, holidaymakers' free time is the working time of local people. This refers to the division of labour in which tourists are the performers and consumers, while local people are the producers. Holidaymakers are not responsible for the working time of local people and workers in tourism.

The commodity-law of value that governs the production system applies to the division of labour in tourism. Local people are able to produce the meaning of a place and local culture in order to attract tourists to visit a place. Thus, the production of meaning and culture is conditioned by the exchange-value of the economic system. This leads to what Baudrillard calls 'the very possibility of production' (1983, p. 97). Human labour and production do not signify the distinctive skills of people and the natural usage of commodity, respectively, although they become exchangeable with money and are subject to the diktats of the market. In terms of local people, to a large extent, they work in constructing meaning and culture in conjunction with global demand and tourist expectations. This is a mere equivalence of agency, not agency itself. The construction of tourist places and tourist objects is, inevitably, dependent upon the demands of the tourist market. Production thus turns out to be equivalence. In addition, both tourists and local people experience alienation in tourism. Putting it at its most extreme, 'The alienation of leisure and tourism relates to the very impossibility of wasting one's times, whereby free time is the freedom to waste one's time but actually is simply the time necessary to reproduce labour power' (Baudrillard 1998, p. 154).

People are unable to waste their time in tourism as that time only allows them to be a productive force. Holidaymakers therefore become labour in producing distinctive value and reproducing the division of working time and free time. Wasting time on holiday is therefore the productive time of the economic system. Local people also become alienated labour in tourism. Tourism is their working time to manufacture tourist objects and create tourist places. The free time of local people is exchangeable with the holiday time of tourists. This is because of the commodity-law of value that regulates the division of time and labour. Although local people can produce the meaning of local culture, they are inextricably subject to global demands and tourist markets. Local people are alienated from what they produce, such as a cultural commodity for sale. In tourism, both tourists and local people appear to be alienated labour.

Baudrillard and globalised tourism

As discussed earlier, the term 'global tourism' emphasises a change in the scale of tourism but gives scant attention to the effect of globalisation on tourism in a local place. I therefore propose the concept of globalised tourism that is developed based on Baudrillard's idea. To define the term 'globalised', we can look at his concept. 'Real globalisation involves a global hyperculture in which the effacing of differences, up to and including what is between the real and the imaginary, annuls also the distance necessary for a relation of identification/distinction' (Baudrillard, in Sassatelli 2002, p. 522).

Like Urry and Meethan, Baudrillard sees 'global' as the flows of cultures and images. The culture of a local place is subject to global flows. Unlike the aforementioned theorists, Baudrillard further elaborates on the effect of globalisation, asserting that it is associated with hyperculture. With globalisation, culture is not there to make a singular difference in each place. Instead, the recreation of culture in a local place for tourists causes the distinction between real culture and contrived/staged culture to disappear. What is globalised in tourism, therefore, refers to the erosion of the difference between real culture and simulated culture.

What is constructed to be sold in tourism appears as real culture. Local people may internalise the effect of globalisation, meaning contrived culture for tourism may later become and act as real, local culture. Additionally, real and traditional local culture is reduced to being an element of simulated culture. This is the stage where tourism in a local place is globalised. In the case studies of Damnoen Saduak and Pattaya Floating Markets, tourism in these places is to some extent globalised, although not entirely. This will be discussed in further chapters.

The circulation of value and signs in the recreation of the floating markets as tourist attractions

In what way are the floating markets tourist attractions? As discussed earlier, the 'other', tourist performances, home/away experience, authenticity and materiality in tourism, are central to understanding tourism. But I would suggest tourism is interwoven with signs. Signs affect our perception of 'others', performance in tourist space and our sense of the place. Material objects are not valued as objects in themselves but as cultural messages. The floating markets do not inherently become tourist attractions, so what is at work in the creation of those places? My research proposes that, with the circulation of value and signs, Damnoen Saduak and Pattaya Floating Markets become tourist attractions.

As Crang says, 'Sacralisation often depends on texts and stories that circulate elsewhere or around the site, so that our sense of having visited somewhere special is premised upon other signs and texts' (Crang 2004, p. 77). A sign is not about the way we gaze upon an object and a place but is a cultural message that values it. Signs transform a place into somewhere to go. In *For a Critique of the Political Economy of the Sign*, Baudrillard introduces the idea that an object of consumption pertains to the logic of significations. Not all objects have sign-value. The sign-object is different from symbolic exchange-value.

Baudrillard says that the object given, or the gift that has symbolic exchange-value, is not autonomous and not codifiable as signs, for it does not depend on economic exchange (Baudrillard 1981, p. 65). The object given has a specific meaning and is associated with the subject who gives the object. For example, a 'thank you' card has symbolic exchange-value that expresses the feeling of appreciation of the giver. The meaning of the card is associated with the giver. It is not exchangeable for money and not codifiable as a sign. The card is thus not a sign-object.

According to Baudrillard,

> the object-become-sign assumes its meaning in its differential relation to other signs. An object is not an object of consumption unless it is released from its physic determinations as a symbol, from its functional determinations as an instrument, from its commercial determinations as a product, and is hence liberated as a sign to be recaptured by the formal logic of fashion.
>
> (Baudrillard 1981, pp. 66–67)

This implies that signs are dependent on economic exchange and must be autonomous from the subjects. A sign-object does not have a specific difference and meaning, for its difference is exchangeable with other signs. Differential signs work in constituting the meaning of objects only when the object disassociates itself from the subject and the context. In other words, what becomes a sign must be context-less, it then opens itself up to relationships with other signs.

For Baudrillard, the meaning of an object is not restricted to the material of the object. The sign-object becomes an object of consumption that does not have physical or functional determinations. It is neither used as a symbol nor as a functional object. It is not used as a commercial product. The sign-object is only used for significations. In the floating market case studies, meanings of places are not inherent attributes. Instead, the markets derive meaning from cultural signs; or rather, what makes the places become tourist attractions is the circulation of value and signs. The stages involving the circulation of value and sign will be introduced now.

Desire and needs

Desire is the first stage of producing value. According to Helgesson and Muniesa, (2013, p. 7), 'Valuation is tied to the conditions of desire and desirability, to the entanglements that are created between people and things, and between people themselves'. The production of value is dependent on desire, and valuation is embedded in the relations between people and things. In this way, valuation is not an inherent attribute of the object, rather it is created socially. Baudrillard elaborated further, stating that both desire and needs accord with market demand. 'Needs can no longer be defined adequately as innate, instinctive power and spontaneous craving. Conversely, they are better defined as a function induced (in the individual) by the internal logic of the system' (Baudrillard 1981, p. 82). Needs are not innate, they are socially constructed. In the floating markets, people's needs are constructed in accordance with tourism. The interaction between the global and the local, together with flows of tourists, constitutes the desire for recreating each floating market.

Use-value and exchange-value

The next stage of the circulation of value and signs is a change in the use-value and exchange-value of Damnoen Saduak and Pattaya Floating Markets. Debates on exchange-value and use-value are now touched upon briefly. Marx and Engels differentiate use-value from exchange-value. They suggest that use-value is the utility of a thing that is limited by the physical properties of the commodity, or what it is used for, whereas exchange-value turns out to be a quantitative relation, meaning the proportion in which values of one sort are exchanged for those of another sort, for example, a quarter of wheat is exchanged for a yard of silk. The exchange of commodities is evidently an act characterised by a total abstraction of use-value (Marx and Engels 1970, pp. 44–45).

For Marx and Engels, the exchange-value of the commodity is independent from use-value, whereby the latter is an intrinsic attribute of the commodity. The differentiation of use-value from exchange-value, which only sees use-value as embedded in the physical property of the commodity, might be insufficient to understand the circulation of value in the floating markets. What becomes commodified is not only subject to exchange-value but also is dissociable from subject and context. As Callon (1999, p. 189) states, 'In order to transform something into a commodity, it is necessary to cut the ties between this thing and other objects or human beings, and this thing must be de-contextualised, dissociated and detached'. A commodity needs to be dissociated from the context in which it is produced and from the subjects who produce it. Only when the thing is freed from context and subjects, is it assigned with economic exchange-value so as to be sold in the market.

What is produced in the market is not only exchange-value but also other forms of use-value. This makes the issue of valuation much more complicated. Goods do not derive value from the market, yet the actor can play an important role in producing value (Vatin 2013, p. 47). To explain this, Vatin proposes,

'All along the chain of production, valorisation is present in acts of evaluation, in that they are provisional modalities for establishing a value that is under construction' (Vatin 2013, p. 45). The act of assessing the value along with that of increasing the value happens simultaneously in the production process. Producers do not only produce goods according to the demand, but they are also able to determine and modify the value of commodities. This appears to contrast with Marx and Engels, who view the production process as unproductive, and the skills of workers as constrained by market demand.

Additionally, Böhme suggests that materiality can manifest itself in three dimensions: physical character, synaesthetic character (aesthetic) and social character. The first refers to the practical and functional dimensions of the material, while the second concerns the character of atmosphere that is perceived through different senses and produced through different material qualities, such as the experience of cold through the colour blue, or the attributes of being warm, gentle, reserved, etc. (Böhme 1995, p. 97). For the third dimension, materials have a social character, through which they can be used for culture and tradition, and this kind of character is presented as a code that must be decoded (Böhme 1995, pp. 97–98). Materials are not only produced for functional application but also for staged value in which they can serve the purposes of aestheticisation and atmosphere, along with culture and tradition.

However, aesthetic value may be dissociable from economic exchange-value, for what becomes exchangeable is aestheticised and vice versa. The two overlap. Baudrillard contends that the use-value of the commodity is dependent on its exchange-value and vice versa. Unlike Marx and Engels, Baudrillard argues, 'Use-value is an abstraction of the system of needs that is cloaked in the false evidence of a concrete destination and purpose, an intrinsic finality of goods and products' (Baudrillard 1981, p. 131). Use-value here does not relate to the needs of people but is socially constructed by the system of production.

> Use-value and exchange-value are controlled by an identical abstract logic of equivalence, an identical code. The code of utility is also a code of abstract equivalence of objects and subjects, and use-value can be fetishised, but not as a practical operation.
>
> (Baudrillard 1981, p. 131)

Both use-value and exchange-value are subject to systems of codes and signs. Use-value is not the practical utility of the object but is subject to differential signs. Hence, use-value is the code of utility.

> In terms of exchange-value, products must be thought of and rationalised in terms of utility in order to be abstractly and generally exchangeable. Therefore, the reduction to the status of utility is the basis of economic exchangeability.
>
> (Baudrillard 1981, p. 131)

In contrast to Marx and Engels, Baudrillard sees exchange-value and use-value as being closely connected with each other. Use-value does not derive from the materiality of the object, or a practical application, instead the code of utility, or the equivalence of use-value, legitimises exchangeability of the objects, and economic exchangeability determines use-value. This generates the system of need along with desire for goods. When use-value is abstract, this triggers fetishism.

The fetishism of code

I think fetishism happens after economic exchangeability has come into play. Economic exchangeability implicitly relates to the commodification process, in which the object is not produced to be used and sold as an object but for its cultural connotation instead. Fetishism is a stage where the production of commodities involves aestheticisation. It is a process that links together exchange-value and use-value with sign-value. Concerning fetishism, Marx and Engels elaborated on this concept.

> The fetishism attaches itself to the products of labour as soon as they are produced as commodities, and the value relation between the products of labour which stamps them as commodities, have absolutely no connection with their physical properties and with the material relations arising therefrom.
>
> (Marx and Engels 1970, p. 77)

The value of commodities is not dependent on their physical properties and human skill. The products of labour do not relate to the needs of labour. They become commodities that are priced and sold in accordance with the exchange-value of the market. Those commodities, in turn, control the needs of humans and the ability of labour. The value of commodities constitutes social relationships between men and between things. For Marx and Engels, labour fetishises the value of the commodities and the exchange-value of the market.

In contrast with Marx, Baudrillard thinks it is insufficient to contextualise fetishism in the contemporary consumption era. Baudrillard further contends,

> By refusing to analyse the structures and the mode of ideological production inherent in its own logic, Marxism is condemned to expand the production of ideology, and the fetishistic theory of infrastructure and superstructure must be replaced by a more comprehensive theory of productive forces, for these are all structurally implicated in the capitalist system, which the concept of fetishism is exploited in an empirical fashion, such as object fetishism, automobile fetishism, vacation fetishism, and so on.
>
> (Baudrillard 1981, pp. 88–90)

For Baudrillard, fetishism does not only involve commodity and money but also other social spheres of everyday life in consumer society. Marx fails to theorise the fetishism that is inherent in the logic of production, and he only views fetishism as ideological. To develop the concept of fetishism, Baudrillard proposes, 'It is not the passion for substances that speaks in fetishism, it is the passion for the code, which by governing both objects and subjects, and by subordinating them to itself, delivers them up to abstract manipulation' (Baudrillard 1981, p. 92).

Baudrillard goes further than Marx and sees the production system as fetishised. Hence, the production of commodities parallels the production of the signifier and the code. Codes that are embedded in objects condition the desires and needs of the subjects. For Baudrillard, fetishism is not only about the passion for an object in exchange for money but also the passion for the code of an object. For example, people do not like Burberry clothes simply because of commodities and value, but rather they are obsessed with the brand – wearing it implies that you have good taste in fashion and it also signifies the affluence of the upper-middle class. People fetishise the codes of production and the code of the object. At the stage of the fetishism of code, sign-value comes into play.

The sign-value turn

According to Baudrillard, the system of value is interrelated with the system of significations and signs due to economic exchangeability. What is produced as commodities has significations. The logic of signs is inherent in the logic of production.

> Ideology has seized all production, material or symbolic, in the same process of abstraction, reduction, general equivalence and exploitation, since the logic of the commodity and of political economy is at the very heart of the sign, in the abstract equation of signifier and signified, in the differential combination of signs, meaning that signs can function as exchange-value (the discourse of communication) and as use-value (rational decoding and distinctive social use).
>
> (Baudrillard 1981, p. 146)

At this stage, exchange-value and use-value are subject to the logic of the sign, whereby the sign turns out to take the form of exchange-value and use-value, and renders exchange-value and use-value generalised and rationalised. Since the logic of the commodity relates to the logic of the sign, exchange-value becomes the discourse of communication that produces the rationalisation of use-value. A sign can function as exchange- and use-value, whereby communicative exchange-value produces social use. The commodities function as a system of communication that regulates exchange-value and use-value. The logic of commodity is equivalent to the logic of the sign. The commodity becomes a code where sign-value can function as exchange-value and use-value. 'Use-value and signified do not have the same weight as exchange-value and signifier respectively. Use-value and needs are only an effect of exchange-value, while signified are only an effect of the signifier' (Baudrillard 1981, p. 137).

Exchange-value refers to the signifier, while use-value refers to the signified. Exchange-value and signifier constitute use-value and signified. Use-value and signified are alibis of exchange-value and signifier, which might mean the latter can be realised in forms of the other two. These are all stages of the circulation of value and signs that enable the floating markets to become tourist attractions.

The production of value and the play of differences

In *The System of Objects*, Baudrillard offers an insightful view on the operation of objects. Referring to Ritzer's 'globalisation of nothing' discussed in the previous chapter, his work may represent the whole strand of globalisation. Although Ritzer's theory enables us to study the cultural content of a tourist place, his criteria are a unidirectional way of approaching global phenomena. Social forms that are endowed with the distincitve cultural content of a place, thing, person and service are 'something', whereas those with indistinctive cultural content appear to be 'nothing'. But can we really separate the original place from the copy? What about staged original content? Do we perceive it as either 'something' or 'nothing'? The differentiation between 'something' and 'nothing' seems to be overdrawn. This is because distinctive cultural content and generic cultural content can overlap. Since the two floating markets regard themselves as authentic, it seems impossible to differentiate one market from the other. The dichotomy of 'something' form and 'nothing' form is thus false. This is because both distinctive and indistinctive cultural contents can be authentic.

To better understand the cultural content of tourist places, Baudrillard's theory will be used to challenge Ritzer. To stress, I do not present Ritzer's approach as a 'straw man' argument, since Ritzer does not place himself in opposition to Baudrillard. Elsewhere, he views the 'nothing' form as similar to Baudrillard's simulation. 'It is "something", that is, it is originals that have distinctive content, whereas all forms of "nothing" are simulations, or copies, which are, by definition, lacking in such content' (Ritzer 2007, p. 94). Globalisation and tourism cause the disappearance of distinctive cultural content, or, rather, cause the emergence of generic culture. However, they are not the same. Distinctive cultural content and generic cultural content can be authentic.

According to Baudrillard,

> the system of differentiation does not operate in terms of real or singular differences between persons, yet what grounds it as a system is precisely the fact that it eliminates the specific content, and substitutes the differential form, which can be industrialised and commercialised as a distinguishing sign.
>
> (Baudrillard 1998, p. 93)

Thus, differences are no longer exclusive, and it is the exchange of differences that clinches group integration, and differences coded in this way become the matter of exchange (Baudrillard 1998, p. 93).

For Baudrillard, there is no singular difference, but the particular content is replaced with differential signs. Differences between each group of people act as distinguishing signs. These are not concrete differences, but the differences function as the matter of exchange or communicative signs. Differences are exchangeable. In contrast with Ritzer, we might not be able to differentiate the cultural content of one object or place from another, since differences are communicative signs rather than functional specificity. In *The System of Objects*, Baudrillard looks at various types of objects, though I only use the elements of his work that are relevant to the floating market case studies, namely 'the non-functional systems' (antique and authenticity) and 'the socio-ideological system of objects' (models/series and the personalised object).

Authenticity

Unlike the aforementioned, Eco states, 'What counts is not the authenticity of a place, yet the amazing information it conveys' (Eco 1998, p. 15). Authenticity is not an inherent attribute, instead it is socially created. Baudrillard also views authenticity as socially constructed rather than as the quest for real culture. Authenticity is not inherently found in an object, place or tradition. Baudrillard thinks authenticity remains enchanting in contemporary society, but he does not place authenticity against pseudo-events and contrived culture as Boorstin does. For Baudrillard, authenticity is the exchange of signification and is embedded in a combination of references. Baudrillard talks about authenticity by looking at an antique object. 'The antique object does not have any practical application and is not functional. On the contrary, it pertains to a very specific function within the system, which is merely to signify, in particular to signify time' (Baudrillard 1996, p. 77).

The existence of some objects does not depend on practical application, yet it responds to other demands, such as witness, nostalgia, etc. These objects are significations of time. Authenticity acts as a differential sign. In addition, Baudrillard stresses,

> No matter how authentic it is, there is always something false about it, and indeed, it is false in so far as it puts itself forward as authentic within a system whose basic principle is by no means authenticity, but rather the calculation of relationships and the abstractness of signs.
>
> (Baudrillard 1996, p. 78)

What becomes authentic is embedded in the relation between the object and subject. Authenticity does not mark that object out as singular and distinctive but, rather, shows the play of differential signs. To stress, authenticity is associated with the antique object.

> The antique object constitutes the mythical evocation of birth in its temporal closure, with beating a path back to the origins meaning regression to

the mother, while the demand for authenticity is reflected in an obsession with certainty as to the origin, date, author and signature of a work. Thus, authenticity always stems from the Father, which is the source of value.

(Baudrillard 1996, pp. 80–81)

We might be unable to mark out the cultural content of the antique object as either distinctive or indistinctive. Instead, the antique object features a sign of origin, which shows regression to the past, and authenticity is the search for value, such as the moment of creation. An object does not intrinsically become authentic but is socially created as authentic, depending on its origin and value. In the case of the two floating markets, authenticity is the important cultural content of the places, which attracts tourists to visit them.

Furthermore, authenticity seems to be enmeshed in the relations between objects and context. As Baudrillard says, 'The quest for authenticity (being-founded-on-itself) is very precisely a quest for an alibi (being-elsewhere)' (Baudrillard 1996, p. 81). Again, authenticity does not inherently occur but depends on the existence of others. Baudrillard uses an article titled *How to Fix Up Your Ruin* as an example, which shows what an architect does with an old farm in Île-de-France (Baudrillard 1996, p. 81). He refers to the presence of a bed-warming pan in an oil-heated house.

> In an oil-heated house, a warming-pan is obviously quite superfluous. If it is not used it will no longer be authentic, it will become a mere cultural sign: the cultural, purposeless warming-pan will emerge as an all-too-faithful image of the vanity of the attempt to retrieve a natural state of affairs by rebuilding this house, and indeed, an all-too-faithful image of the architect himself who has no part to play here, since his entire social existence lies elsewhere; his very being is elsewhere. For him, nature is nothing but a cultural luxury.
>
> (Baudrillard 1996, p. 83)

The quest for authenticity seems to be the quest of others whose presence does not fit in that context, as seen in the example of the warming pan (outdated style) in an oil-heated house (modern style). An authentic object must be used to serve some purpose, albeit being present in an irrelevant context. Why does an authentic object need to be used? The search for authenticity is the search for an alibi that implicitly refers to the co-existence of a functional object with a mythological object in one context.

> A functional object that configures the loss of Father and the Mother is rich in functionality yet impoverished in meaning, whereby its frame of reference is the present moment and its possibilities do not extend beyond everyday life.
>
> (Baudrillard 1996, pp. 85–86)

A functional object does not inherently have meaning, but that does not mean the object has no meaning at all. The existence of a functional object is tied to its present context. A functional object is thus born with the loss of meaning and value. 'In contrast, the mythological object has minimal function and maximal meaning, while its frame of reference is the ancestral realm – perhaps even the realm of the absolute anteriority of nature' (Baudrillard 1996, p. 86).

The cultural content of the mythological object is embedded in the realm of tradition. A mythological object might have a practical application, but what significantly constitutes its existence is that it is rich in meaning. A mythological object dissociates itself from its context. The existence of the object should have appeared elsewhere, where the signifying of its value or origin would be evident. Although the object must be used to serve a purpose in order to become authentic, the usage of the mythological object does not endow it with a practical application. Rather, its usage depends on the existence of functional objects in the same context.

Baudrillard stresses, 'On the plane of direct experience, the antithetical traits of the mythological and the functional can co-exist in complementary fashion within one system, for instance, the architect has a peasant-style warming-pan in the oil-heated house' (Baudrillard 1996, p. 86). The mythological and the functional attributes of the object can co-present in a complementary way in one system. Although the mythological object has minimal function, it has maximal meaning, which may associate it with the realm of tradition or the myth of origin. To ensure its being, the mythological object searches for the existence of the functional object and vice versa. In other words, the search for authenticity is the search for an alibi that lies in another object. Constructing authenticity is dependent on the relations between objects and context. Authenticity involves both social usage and a sign (value).

Series object

Apart from authenticity, the play of differences can be found in series objects. Some places or objects tend to be inessentially different from others, whereby they pertain to a model and a series of dynamics, or a socio-ideological system. Baudrillard notes,

> The psycho-sociological dynamic of a model and series does not operate at the level of the object's primary function, but only at the level of a secondary function, at the level of the personalised object. That is to say, at the level of an object grounded simultaneously in individual requirements and in that system of differences that is the cultural system itself.
>
> (Baudrillard 1996, p. 51)

Model and series do not rely on the objective function; rather, the personalisation function that involves the cultural system. Personalisation does not mark one object out as distinctive, for the difference does not depend on practical application. The object pertains to differential sign (value).

Regarding personalisation and integration, Baudrillard articulates, 'The model is discernible everywhere in the series, with the status of a model showing relative differences, which refers to how all the others create the idea of absolute difference' (Baudrillard 1996, pp. 154–155).

A model presents relative differences between the series but integrates all series. Each series can refer back to the model. Again, this is not a singularity or specific difference. Model and series are differential signs that are a matter of exchange. In terms of cultural nostalgia, the model/series dynamic can also come into play. A series object can also refer to serial time.

> Apart from a loss of uniqueness of style, the series stands also for the loss of the real dimension of time which is located not exactly in the present, but instead in an immediate past, and serial time is always the time of the wave before, whereby most people live in a time that is not theirs, a time of generality, of insignificance, a time that is not modern but not yet antique.
>
> (Baudrillard 1996, pp. 163–164)

Establishing value that relates to past tradition is another form of series. Serial time thus dissociates itself from the real dimension of time in that it does not pertain to the present time or the past. Serial time, as differential signs, becomes inessential time used to create inessential content and personalised difference.

The cultural consequences of globalisation: simulacrum

Some theorists finalise the cultural consequences of globalisation and tourism, or think globalisation and tourism lead to different ends of culture, as seen in the following examples. Do globalisation and tourism lead to homogenisation? Ritzer and Liska (1997, p. 98) propose the 'McDisneyization' of the tourist industry, where tourist attractions not only look more like a Disney theme park but also embrace the four basic principles of McDisneyization: efficiency, calculability, predictability and non-human technology (1997, p. 98). For Ritzer and Liska, tourist attractions engage with the McDisneyization processes that trigger a standardised, or homogenised, tourist experience.

Similar to Ritzer and Liska, Bryman (2003, pp. 154–155) introduces the term 'Disneyization', which refers to Disney theme parks, and all other theme parks modelled on them, as providing predictable tourist entertainment and exerting considerable control over their guests, such as through the use of non-human technology, and that those theme parks are highly efficient in their processing of guests.

Bryman uses Disney theme parks to exemplify patterned tourist places and standardised tourist experiences. Predictable tourist activities, together with efficient tourist services, may be necessary to enable tourist attractions to meet travellers' expectations, but can we separate homogenisation from diversification? Diversification may be a homogenised tourist experience. For instance, Damnoen Saduak and Pattaya Floating Markets, which have both become popular tourist attractions, offer different packages of Thai culture, namely, local Thai culture and four regional Thai cultures. Although the floating markets are patterned tourist experiences, they offer different packages of Thai culture. Therefore, in the case of these two floating markets, homogenisation and diversification overlap.

In contrast to homogenisation, Lash and Urry (1994, p. 273) argue that, 'The mass holiday in which all customers were treated as relatively similar has declined in popularity'. The two floating markets do not provide tourists with a mass holiday, but one of the floating markets might specifically respond to a different group of tourists. For instance, Pattaya Floating Market is orientated towards Chinese tourists, and thus Thai culture is tailor-made for them. The effect of globalisation is not homogenised but instead varies according to the locale. As Baudrillard states, globalisation is homogenised yet fragmented. Therefore, we may not be able to finalise the cultural consequence of globalisation as glocalisation, and hybridisation. 'Baudrillard's analysis is not a matter of the disappearance of differences, rather the erosion of their strength and their reciprocal incommensurability' (Sassatelli 2002, p. 521).

Globalisation does not trigger the disappearance of different social and cultural forms. Rather, with globalisation, social forms and cultural forms become exchangeable and replaceable with one another. Instead of finalising the cultural consequence of globalisation, I suggest that globalisation leads to simulation. Simulation is not a new concept. Another theorist whose work parallels Baudrillard's is Eco, as seen in the collection of essays, *Travels in Hyperreality*. Eco uses America to exemplify hyperreality. 'America enters hyperreality in search of instances where the American imagination demands the real thing and, to attain it, must fabricate the absolute fake, meaning falsehood is enjoyed in a situation of fullness' (Eco 1998, p. 8).

The absolute fake turns out to be the real and acts as the real. Although Eco's viewpoint is generally similar to Baudrillard, Baudrillard is more pessimistic. Baudrillard does not see the fake as the real and does not even use the word 'fake' in opposition to the real. For Baudrillard, simulation is not about the fake becoming the real. This is because the fake can imitate the real, yet simulation is not about imitating the real. Instead, it becomes the real itself. As Baudrillard states, 'Simulacrum involves substituting signs of the real for the real itself; that is, an operation to deter every real process by its operational double, whereas simulation threatens the difference between true and false, between real and imaginary' (Baudrillard 1983, pp. 4–5).

Simulation is not about being a copy, or fake; if it is a copy or duplication, the difference between the real and the false is still apparent. A copy that tries to imitate the real does not, and never will, become the real, as is the case, for example, with a real iPhone and a fake one. We are able to tell the difference between these two objects although they look alike, because a fake iPhone might not function properly, or it might differ in colour from the real one. Unlike a copy, simulation attempts to devour the real. Signs of the real eclipse the real so as to become the real itself. The difference between the real and unreal becomes blurred, or even irrelevant. Simulation corrupts the original, whereby the purpose of the original becomes exchangeable with, and substituted for, signs.

In *Simulations*, Baudrillard proposes three orders of appearance running parallel to the mutations of the law of value, including counterfeit, production and simulation (Baudrillard 1983, p. 83). In addition, the way Baudrillard talks about the orders of simulacra distinguishes him further from Eco, in that Baudrillard views simulation as a process that causes changes in contemporary society.

Baudrillard proposes that, in the first order of simulacrum, based on the natural law of value, counterfeit (and fashion at the same time) is born with the destructuring of the feudal order by the bourgeois order and the emergence of open competition on the level of the distinctive sign (1983, pp. 83–84).

In the first order of simulacrum, the sign that used to tie in with social class and mark a specific meaning in the age of feudalism and ancient culture is no longer restricted to the realm of traditional culture. It is de-traditionalised and free from its own realm.

> This marks the end of the obliged sign and the beginning of the reign of the emancipated sign, with us passing from a limited order of signs to a proliferation of signs, according to demand. The first-order of simulacrum never abolishes the difference, rather it presupposes an always detectable dispute between semblance and reality.
>
> (Baudrillard 1983, pp. 85, 94–95)

The sign becomes arbitrary, in that the signifier does not refer to the specific signified. The capitalist economic system, along with market demand, bolsters the proliferation of signs. Signs of the object, and of the tourist places, are modified and reconstructed in globalisation and tourism. Simulation does not make original local culture disappear; rather, the existence of the original culture depends on simulation. Original culture is one of the elements of simulation. In the first order of simulacrum, the counterfeit still displays reference to the real. In contrast to the first order of simulacrum, the third order of simulacrum sees the emergence of the hyperreal in which signs of the real become more real.

> Here it is a question of a reversal of origin and finality, for all the forms change once they are not so much mechanically reproduced but even conceived from the point of view of their very reproducibility, diffracted from a generating nucleus we call the model. Here we are in the third-order simulacra, playing with the structural law of value, and here are the models from which proceed all forms according to the modulation of their differences.
>
> (Baudrillard 1983, pp. 100–101)

In the third order of simulacrum, it is not about the disappearance of the real, rather it is that the real can be generated and reproduced indefinitely. This stage is marked out with a reversal of origin and finality. The real is not fixed but deconstructed and reconstructed according to the model. The model of the real and sign of the real that substitute the real turn out to produce social forms. This leads to the precession of simulacra – 'Simulation is the generation by models of a real without origin or reality. For instance, the territory no longer precedes the map, instead the map comes to precede the territory, or it is the map that engenders the territory' (Baudrillard 1983, p. 2). Simulacrum generates the real, which does not bear any relation to the original.

Simulation and media

Moreover, the third order of simulacrum is the stage at which the media plays an important role in reconstructing and disseminating reality. Concerning film tourism, Buchmann, Moore and Fisher interestingly propose the following: 'Film tourism has two layers of complexity that combine representations, simulations and contrivances with real-world travel to specific destinations that are either associated with the production of a film or have been depicted in a film' (2010, p. 233). Although what we see in a film is a representation and constructed image, corporeal travel enables us to experience the real place. It implies simulated travel is a supplement to corporeal travel to the real place and vice versa. However, in some cases, film or the media do not represent reality, rather they recreate reality.

Baudrillard highlights that today both objects and information resulting from a selection and a point of view have broken down reality into simple elements that they have reassembled into scenarios of regulated oppositions (Baudrillard 1983, p. 120).

In this case, the media do not produce the real. Rather, reality is selected to be presented via the media. What we see is the mediated reality. Reality can be rearranged into different scenarios.

The deterrence model

Another element of the third order of simulacrum is the deterrence model. Baudrillard notes that 'hyperreality and simulation are deterrents of every principle and every objective, they turn against power the deterrent that it used so well for such a long time' (1994, p. 22). Deterrence means inability to access the real. Baudrillard discusses Disneyland and Beaubourg[1] as examples of the deterrence model. Baudrillard is not the first person to discuss Disneyland in this way, however. Eco also perceives Disneyland as hyperreal, in that he regards Disneyland as a falsified experience. Disneyland can present its reconstructions as masterpieces of falsification, for what it sells is genuine merchandise, not reproductions, but what is falsified is our will to buy, which we take as real (Eco 1998, p. 43). Disneyland is the absolute fake that reproduces the real, and what is presented there is falsification. Although the goods that are sold there are real, our needs for those goods are false, and the value of them is fabricated. We go to Disneyland and purchase goods because they are Disneyland items, not items themselves. In this case, an object is not valued as an object but rather decoded to give a cultural message.

Despite being a falsified place, Disneyland does not become the real for beyond Disneyland lies the real country. Again, a falsified experience for Eco is not the same as a hyperreal experience for Baudrillard, although they are very close. To elaborate further than Eco, a hyperreal experience causes a reversal of origin, and it acts as deterrent that even denies us the ability to access the real. Disneyland is the totality of culture. On Disneyland, it

> ... is there to conceal the fact that it is the real country, all of real America, which is Disneyland. It is presented as imaginary so as to make us believe that the rest is real, when in fact all of Los Angeles and the America surrounding it are no longer real, but of the order of the hyperreal and of simulation.
>
> (Baudrillard 1983, p. 25)

This implies an inverse relationship between Disneyland and America, where Disneyland turns out to represent the real country and America is not real. There is also a reversal of origin, whereby America, the real country, becomes the simulacrum of Disneyland. In other words, miniaturised units of Disneyland constitute the reality of America. 'The Disneyland imaginary is neither true nor false, instead it is a deterrence machine set up in order to rejuvenate in reverse the fiction of the real' (Baudrillard 1983, p. 25). We cannot see Disneyland as either true or false, for the distinction between true and false is unclear. Disneyland as a deterrence model causes a reverse of reality; hence, any access to reality is impossible.

Apart from Disneyland, another deterrence model, called the Beaubourg-Effect, is illustrated in Baudrillard's work.

> The whole social discourse is there, and both on this level and that of cultural manipulation, Beaubourg, the space of deterrence, is – in total contradiction to its staged objectives – a brilliant monument to modernity.
>
> (Baudrillard 1994, pp. 4 and 62)

> Granted, the entire cultural contents of Beaubourg are anachronistic, since only an interior void could have corresponded to this architectural envelope. The culture itself is dead. One should have erected a monument, or anti-monument, equivalent to the phallic inanity of the Eiffel Tower.
>
> (Baudrillard 1982, p. 4)

As a deterrence model, Beaubourg does not only deter attempts to access the real culture, but it also causes the real culture to be neutralised. This is a further stage of the hyperreal. Beaubourg looks like a cultural centre that absorbs all of its surroundings and surrounding culture, which leads to the destruction of all its cultural contents. The place produces social discourse by manipulating culture. Its cultural contents are anachronistic. The incongruence of its cultural contents, especially the reconstruction of the Eiffel Tower in Beaubourg/the Centre Georges Pompidou, makes the place become a total creation (hyperreal). For Beaubourg, each order of the simulacra does not exist independently but interrelates with the others. The alibi of a preceding order maintains the existence of a subsequent order and a preceding order, giving cultural meaning to the empty substance of the subsequent one (Baudrillard 1982, p. 6).

Furthermore, the process of simulation produces the masses.

> One invites the masses to participate, to simulate, and to play with the models – they go one better: they participate and manipulate so well that they efface all the meaning. Thus, they become hypersimulated in response to cultural simulation and, in turn, become the agents of the execution of this culture.
>
> (Baudrillard 1994, p. 66)

The masses come to see and enjoy simulation of culture. Their participation in cultural simulation erodes the meaning of culture. Their response to cultural simulation is thus simulation of action. This is because what is produced is not a real social form but a simulated version. The deterrence model and simulation affect the agency of people. Hyperreality and the deterrence model lead to what Baudrillard calls 'the production of the masses' (1994, p. 68). 'The masses are the increasingly dense sphere in which the whole social comes to be imploded, and to be devoured in an uninterrupted process of simulation' (Baudrillard 1994, p. 68). Orders of simulacra, along with the process of simulation, produce social forms that the masses must follow, and Baudrillard believes they are happy to do so. Action of the masses maintains the process of simulation, while simulation produces social forms and meaning for the masses. Therefore, simulation is indefinitely reproduced in contemporary society.

Conclusion and critiques of Baudrillard

Although Baudrillard's theory on leisure enables us to understand the impacts of the economic system on tourism, one important point remains unclear. Baudrillard (1998, p. 157) states, 'Free time that is economically unproductive is the time of a production of value'.

But is free time in tourism really economically unproductive? If this is the case, why does tourism generate a considerable amount of income for a destination country, and what feeds on the production of local culture? Tourists must pay for free time on holiday. In this manner, they can trigger economically productive labour that facilitates flows of capital in tourism. Tourist expenditure enables local people to produce, and reproduce, a tourist place and a tourist object. Tourists do not want to do anything productive during their holidays, yet paradoxically they may provide economically productive labour. Baudrillard's theory is a one-sided take on structure that happens to influence agency, while his theory does not allow us to see how agency reflexively constitutes social form and structure.

In addition, Gottdiener (in Sandywell 1995, p. 146) talks of a journey towards reductionism in pursuit of an extreme vision – the reduction of all life to the hyperreal in the culture of postmodernity. For Baudrillard, people's everyday life involves a hyperreal version of culture. People can only access representation of culture or simulacrum of culture. He denies the existence of real culture, since culture is commodified when it encounters the capitalist economy and global flows. In this manner, culture is regarded as a consumption process.

However, Baudrillard does not take the dynamics of culture into account. Culture is not static but subject to change, according to other external forces, such as virtual identity, the media, power or authority. It may also be subject to internal forces, whereby people can modify and adapt their culture to global flows so that their culture can exist in a current context. To understand the dynamics of culture, we can look back at Hannerz's cosmopolitanism, for example, which emphasises cultural diversity (Hannerz 2004).[2] People are able to experience other cultures while preserving their own in a changing context.

Regarding the orders of simulacra, it is not clear how these orders are developed and how the system of simulation is sustained. As Sandywell (1995, p. 133) contends, 'Baudrillard is vague about these historical and sociological linkages, and the dynamic connections between simulacral orders and epochal systems are left untheorised'. Baudrillard does not state explicitly how each order of simulacrum connects with different historical periods. Thus, it remains unclear how each order of simulacrum overlaps in contemporary society.

Notes

1 'Beaubourg centres on the Centre Pompidou, and it is one of the most city's popular and recognisable landmarks, and one of the twentieth century's most radical buildings' (Rough Guide 2018).
2 Please refer back to chapter 2 on globalisation.

References

Baudrillard, J. (1981). *For a Critique of the Political Economy of the Sign*. Trans. C. Levin. St. Louis, MO: Telos Press.

Baudrillard, J. (1982). The Beaubourg-Effect: Implosion and Deterrence. Trans. by R. Krauss and A. Michelson. *October*, 20, 3–13.

Baudrillard, J. (1983). *Simulations*. Trans. P. Foss, P. Patton, and P. Beitchman. Los Angeles, CA: Semiotext(e).

Baudrillard, J. (1994). *Simulacra and Simulation*. Trans. S.F. Glaser. Ann Arbor, MI: The University of Michigan Press.

Baudrillard, J. (1996). *The Systems of Objects*. Trans. J. Benedict. London: Verso.

Baudrillard, J. (1998). *The Consumer Society Myths and Structures*. London: Sage.

Baudrillard, J. (2003). *The Violence of the Global* [Online]. Trans. F. Debrix. Available from: https://journals.uvic.ca/index.php/ctheory/article/view/14558/5403. [Accessed 1 April 2017].

Böhme, G. (1995). Staged Materiality. *Diadalos*, 56, 36–43.

Bryman, A. (2003). McDonald's as a Disneyized Institution: Global Implications. *American Behavioral Scientist*, 47(2), 154–167.

Buchmann, A., Moore, K. and Fisher, D. (2010). Experiencing Film Tourism: Authenticity and Fellowship. *Annals of Tourism Research*, 37(1), 229–248.

Callon, M. (1999). Actor-Network Theory – The Market Test. *The Sociological Review*, 47(S1), 181–195.

Crang, M. (2004). Cultural Geographies of Tourism. In: A.A. Lew, M. Hall and A.M. Williams (eds), *A Companion to Tourism*. Oxford: Blackwell Publishing Ltd, pp. 74–84.

Eco, U. (1998). *Faith in Fakes: Travels in Hyperreality*. London: Vintage.

Hannerz, U. (2004). Cosmopolitanism. In: D. Nugent and J. Vincent (eds), *A Companion to the Anthropology of Politics*. Oxford: Blackwell Publishing Ltd, pp. 69–86.

Helgesson, C.F. and Muniesa, F. (2013). For What It's Worth: An Introduction to Valuation Studies. *Valuation Studies*, 1(1), 1–10.

Lash, S. and Urry, J. (1994). *Economies of Signs and Space*. London: Sage.

Martinelli, A. (2003). Global Order or Divided World? Introduction. *Current Sociology*, 51(2), 95–100.

Marx, K. and Engels, F. (1970). *Capital: A Critique of Political Economy Capitalist Production*, Vol. 1. London: Lawrence & Wishart.

Ritzer, G. (2007). *The Globalization of Nothing 2*. Thousand Oaks, CA: Pine Forge Press.

Ritzer, G. and Liska, A. (1997). McDisneyization and Post-Tourism: Complementary Perspectives on Contemporary Tourism. In: C. Rojek and J. Urry (eds), *Touring Cultures: Transformations of Travel and Theory*. Abingdon: Routledge, pp. 96–109.

Rough Guides (2018). Beaubourg and Around. [Online]. Available from: www.roughguides.com/destinations/europe/france/paris/beaubourg-around/. [Accessed 15 May 2018].

Sandywell, B. (1995). Review Article: Forget Baudrillard. *Theory, Culture & Society*, 12(4), 125–152.

Sassatelli, M. (2002). An Interview with Jean Baudrillard: Europe, Globalization and the Destiny of Culture. *European Journal of Social Theory*, 5(4), 521–530.

Vatin, F. (2013). Valuation as Evaluating and Valorizing. *Valuation Studies*, 1(1), 31–50.

5 Circulation of value and sign

Introduction

Damnoen Saduak and Pattaya Floating Markets did not spontaneously occur, nor did they naturally become tourist attractions. Rather, they are tourist-orientated places, and the utilities of those places are subject to economic exchange-value and sign-value induced by tourism. Referring to Chapter 4, holiday time in the floating markets is non-working time for tourists, yet it is not free. It depends on economic exchange-value, with tourists having to pay for services as well as an admission fee.

This chapter investigates in what ways the markets have become tourist attractions. I suggest that it is the circulation of value and signs that works to create the tourist-orientated markets and stages of representation, though they are tourist attractions in different ways. Damnoen Saduak Floating Market has changed from being a site of local water trading to a tourist site, whereas Pattaya Floating Market is a tourist-orientated market that has been gradually developed and expanded over time. Baudrillard's theory of political economy of signs will be employed to analyse how the circulation of value and signs has transformed the floating markets into tourist-orientated places.

The purpose of the floating markets

This theme derives from an interview question that asked, 'How did the floating market occur?' Looking first at Damnoen Saduak Floating Market, it was commissioned to be excavated and built in 1866, during the reign of King Rama IV in order to connect with the Tha Jean and Mae Klong rivers in adjacent provinces in the west of Thailand. The canal was completed in 1868 during the reign of King Rama V and named Damnoen Saduak Canal, which translates as 'convenient transportation' in Thai. The canal is 32km long and links with 200 other small canals. The first purpose of the canal was transportation, when boats were the main mode of getting around. Living by the canals formed a riparian way of life, especially water trading, resulting in a floating market where local people came to sell and exchange local produce. The floating market has existed for more than 100 years; interviewees said they could not remember exactly, but it was a very long time ago.

Before relocating to the roadside, tourists were only able to access the floating market by boat. Rowers collected tourists at the bus stop and ferried them to the market. One interviewee said 'I'm not sure when tourists first visited the market. I have seen tourists there since I was born' (Ms. Wang# n=22# female# Damnoen Saduak). From the interview data, the occurrence of water trading and the floating market at first related to the physical location since it was surrounded by canals; also, boat transportation and the canals facilitated floating markets to emerge, so that local people could exchange and sell produce to each other. Damnoen Saduak Floating Market saw an increase in the number of tourists after the market was relocated to another area of the canal.

As Pongajarn, Van der Duim and Peters (2016, p. 5) assert, the floating market changed its location from the Ludpee canal to the Tonkem canal in a non-residential area, which has been accessible by road since 1972. The relocated market is now next to the main road, making it more convenient for tourists travelling to the market by car. Road construction means that cars have become the main mode of transport for tourists and local people, and has thus replaced water transportation. This was the first stage of the global reshaping of desires and needs for a floating market. Needs are not innate, they are socially constructed.

Regarding Pattaya Floating Market, the place is a tourist attraction constructed and run by a private owner. It has a different purpose from its previous incarnation. Informants stated,

ME: Could you tell me how did the market started?
INTERVIEWEE: The floating market was constructed in 2008. Prior to the construction of the floating market, this place was a natural swamp, and Mr. A owned this land. He wanted to see Thai boat vendors like it was in the old days.
(Mr. B# n=1# male# Pattaya)

I also interviewed Mr. A about the establishment of the market.

ME: How did you get involved in the tourism business?
INTERVIEWEE: I came from Ayutthaya city [80km north of Bangkok, and the capital of Thailand about 250 years ago]. I often went abroad and thought about what I wanted to see in each country. In Thailand, there were many stories that we did not pay attention to and didn't value them. Why didn't we present our Thai way of life or our identity? When tourists come here, they might want to see Thainess, but they did not have the chance to view it in Pattaya. For tourists, Pattaya city was popular for entertainment and nightlife. I wanted to change this by displaying the Thai way of life in Pattaya. I decided to build the first privately owned floating market in Thailand. I looked at the original floating markets, such as Amphawa and Damnoen Saduak, places that used to be part of the way of life in the past. But the nature of those places has been changed by the arrival of tourists, especially group tours, meaning the old way of life has disappeared. So I focused on presenting the Thai way of life in [Pattaya] market. (Mr. A# n=8# male# Pattaya)

According to the interview data, on the one hand, the desire and need for Pattaya Floating Market came from the nostalgic idea of Mr. A who wanted to see Thai boat vendors as it was in the old days, and he thought the original floating markets had changed. On the other hand, globalisation and tourism had brought about the desire for the floating market, as the owner said, 'Tourists do not have the opportunity to see the Thai way of life in Pattaya'. The market thus presents the Thai way of life that he thought tourists might want to see. Again, the need for Pattaya Floating Market was not innate but socially constructed.

Referring back to Baudrillard, the needs of people are not innate but rather are subject to the regulation of the economic system, of which he states, 'There are only needs because the system needs them' (Baudrillard 1981, p. 81). People's needs are socially constructed by market demand, and this enables the continued existence of the capitalist economy. In the case of the two floating markets, tourist arrivals facilitated the re-creation of Damnoen Saduak Floating Market, whereas nostalgia for the Thai way of life, along with the arrival of tourists, shaped the need for a floating market in Pattaya city. The needs of tourism influenced the needs of local people to construct the floating markets. The social construction of needs makes globalisation and tourism prevalent – this paves the way for the next stage: that the markets are tourist sites because of the circulation of value.

Forms of exchange-value and use-value

We need to study the form of value in the two floating markets as it will enable us to see how sign-value eclipses exchange-value and use-value at a later stage. For Baudrillard, economic exchange-value determines the use-value of the object. In this case, the exchange-value of the floating markets is derived from the opposing gaze upon tourists as the 'other'. Employing the opposing gaze, Damnoen Saduak Floating Market uses different pricing of goods for tourists, whereas Pattaya Floating Market collects an admission fee from foreign tourists.

Economic exchangeability refers to 'commission and price for foreign tourists', which implies unequal flows of cash between the global (tourists) and local. At Damnoen Saduak Floating Market, workers refer to foreign tourists as 'them'. Foreign walk-in tourists, or foreign group tours, have to pay for rowing-boat services. Each boat service pays wages to their rowers (employees), while traders pay rent to the boat-services owner and commission a rower if they bring tourists to their floating shop houses where tourists may then purchase things. A boat-service owner pays commission to a tour guide (group tours) or a taxi driver (walk-in tourists). Boat-ride services involving economic exchange are useful for taking tourists around the market. A boat ride is exchangeable with a fee. Thus, economic exchangeability determines the code of utility of boat-ride services. Economic exchangeability affects their local workers' views of tourists and their uses of the floating market.

We do not use price tags here, as we offer different prices for foreigners and Thai tourists, in that we expect them [foreign tourists] to pay a more expensive price than the Thai tourists do, as the first group has more money for travelling, so they should pay a higher price.

(Ms. Aey# n=29# female# Damnoen Saduak)

ME: Are most tourists here foreigners?

INTERVIEWEE: Yes, we have cheap tours visiting the market from June to August, and expensive/rich tours coming here from November to December.

ME: What do you mean by 'cheap tour' and 'rich tour'?

INTERVIEWEE: Cheap tours are tourists who buy nothing in the market, just sight-see. But rich tours [are tourists who] buy lots of souvenirs, [spending] up to 10,000 baht (about £232.00).

ME: How do you know the difference between these two groups?

INTERVIEWEE: The tour guides tell us what grades/types of tourists they are.
(Ms. Aey# n=29# female# Damneon Saduak)

Workers also used the terms 'Thai price' or 'foreigner price' to differentiate between Thai tourists and foreigners.

We are not able to ask for high prices with Thai tourists because Thais know [if they are too high] and refuse to buy things. Thai and foreign tourists pay a different fee for the boat-ride service, which costs 450 baht (about £4.00) for a one-hour rowing-boat ride for Thai tourists, whereas it costs 600–650 baht (about £13.00) for foreigners.

(Ms. Aey# n=29# female# Damnoen Saduak)

Another example of 'Thai price' and 'foreigner price' is shown as follows:

ME: If I bought this product [made from coconuts], how much would it cost?

INTERVIEWEE: I would sell it to you for 90 baht [about £1.50–£2.00].

ME: But how much would you sell this for to foreign tourists?

INTERVIEWEE: Perhaps 500 baht [about £11.60]. We don't use price tags because of price haggling. Some items are sold for 500 baht, but they [tourists] sometimes only offer to pay 50 baht [about £1]. (Ms. Pam# n=21# female# Damnoen Saduak)

Due to the status of the utility of the floating market being subject to the economic exchange-value, or unequal flows of cash, Damnoen Saduak Floating Market is definitely a tourist attraction. The boat-ride service is useful because it can be exchangeable with money. Hence, use-value does not relate to the physical place. In the case of Damnoen Saduak Floating Market, use-value is not different from exchange-value, as it implies the economic exchangeability with income from tourists.

Regarding Pattaya Floating Market, it was created as a tourist attraction where the exchange-value is generalised and use-value is abstract. The use-value of

Pattaya Floating Market does not relate to its physical location, a natural swamp, but rather to the economic exchange due to tourism. The economic exchange-value of Pattaya Floating Market refers to the admission fee, commission, rent and salary. The floating market becomes a tourist attraction because of the admission fee.

When tourists arrive at the market, there are two entrances: the first one, which has 'We are Thai, free entry' written in Thai over it, is only for Thai tourists; the other one, where 'Entrance' is written in English, is for foreign tourists, who have to pay 200 baht (about £4.00) for admission. Traders pay rent to the market, and the market pays commission to tour guides and salaried staff. Similar to Damnoen Saduak Floating Market, foreigners are regarded as 'others' or 'them'. So why do foreign tourists have to pay an admission fee, while it is free for Thai tourists? The following interviews may explain this.

ME: I had heard from TripAdvisor that some foreign tourists were not happy with the admission fee. What did you think about this?

INTERVIEWEE: At the entrance, there is a sign written in Thai, saying, 'We are Thai, free entry'. When you travel abroad and visit a church, you pay an admission fee, right? So, when you [foreign tourists] visit my place, we ask you to pay a cover charge. What's wrong with that? You visit my country, you have to pay. If not, what is the point of having a visa? (Mr. A# n=8# male# Pattaya)

Workers see foreigners as 'them' or 'others', so the market requires them to pay an admission fee. The emergence of the market depends on the admission fee.

Admission fees are economic exchanges that constitute the status of utility of the market. The economic exchange-value of the floating markets produces the code of utility, and the circulation of value enables the market to be a tourist-orientated place.

Having presented a form of exchange-value, a form of use-value will be presented in the next section.

Staged culture (use-value)

Baudrillard uses the term 'the code of utility' to show how the use-value is socially constructed in accordance with the economic exchange-value. In this case, the code of utility refers to staged culture. The use-value of the two floating markets accords with the economic exchange-value. Use-value is not inherent in an object or place as Marx and Engels propose, yet it is implicated in the relationship of workers with tourism. In this section, we will see how exchange-value takes the form of use-value. People do not need objects because they are useful objects, but rather because of the code of the object. Therefore, both use-value and exchange-value are abstract and turn out to be equivalence.

To exemplify this stage, the staged-culture sub-theme will be presented. In this context, staged culture refers to made-up culture that becomes the code of utility of the markets and justifies the floating markets as tourist attractions. For Damnoen Saduak Floating Market, the place was formerly an actual market where local people, dressed in fruit farmers' clothes, came to sell and exchange local produce. Interviewees said 'the construction of the boat service replaces some local people's houses. There used to be wooden houses alongside the canal' (Ms. Nat# n=24# female# Damnoen Saduak). Since Damnoen Saduak Floating Market entered tourism, and globalisation, use-value has become abstract and, thus, equivalence of exchange-value. As previously stated, the market was relocated to another side of the canal because of road construction. Boats are no longer the main mode of transportation; rather, they are reduced to a code of utility that helps the floating market function as a tourist-orientated place which seeks to meet tourist expectations.

> Some boat vendors travel to the market by car, then transfer to rowing boats that are stationed at different positions along the canal so as to act as floating vendors. Vendors come here by car as they want to avoid boat traffic with tourist boats on the canals. It's easier for them to use a car.
>
> (Ms. Pam# n=21# female# Damnoen Saduak)

In addition, the market changed its opening times.

> In the past, fruit farmers started selling produce before dawn and finished in the morning (9/10am). But now the opening times have changed for tourist arrivals, starting from 9–9.30am to 12 or 1pm.
>
> (Ms. C# n=28# female# Damnoen Saduak)

Based on the interview data, the functionality of Damnoen Saduak Floating Market is abstract, with its opening times being dependent on tourist arrivals, and floating vendors coming to the market by car, not only to sell produce and other things but also to act as floating vendors. The use-value and the existence of the floating market depend on tourism. The opening times are helpful for tourists who come to see the market in action. Also, since the construction of the road, boats have been replaced by cars. Boat transportation turns out to be a code of utility that enables vendors to act as floating vendors, meaning the use-value is the equivalence of exchange-value and vice versa. As a constructed market, the use-value of Pattaya Floating Market is also abstract. The function of boats in Pattaya Floating Market does not relate to its material properties, or objective function, instead they have become a mere code of utility,

> We [Pattaya Floating Market] provide our traders with rowing boats, though the traders don't row them. Boats are stationed at different positions and floating vendors don't travel around the market. All they need to do is just sit on the rowing boats to sell food, namely roti, noodles, grilled-fish balls and the like.
>
> (Mr. Sam# n=3# male# Pattaya)

The use-value of boats in Pattaya Floating Market does not appear to relate to its material properties (using boats for transportation), or to have a connection with the subjects at all. The below is an example.

> At first, sitting in a rowing boat was tough and uncomfortable, but I got used to it. It took me, like, a week to manage to sit on the boat. It doesn't wobble that much now.
>
> (Ms. Som# n=14# female# Pattaya)

The code of utility of boats in Pattaya Floating Market enables vendors to perform authentically as floating vendors in order for the place to become a floating market. This is because a floating vendor is one of the important components of a floating market. Pattaya Floating Market provides some traders with rowing boats. The utility of rowing boats is determined by economic exchange, including commission, admission fee and income, from tourists. Therefore, floating vendors and rowing boats here are examples of a staged culture that is orientated towards tourists, and their use-value is dependent on the economic exchangeability of tourism.

Regarding its opening times, Pattaya Floating Market is open from 9am to 8pm,

> Foreign tourists, especially group tours, arrive in the market from 4pm to 7pm, but Thai tourists usually come here from 12pm to 4pm.
>
> (Mr. Nat# n=9# male# Pattaya)

The opening times of the market are dependent on the arrival of tourists. In this way, Pattaya Floating Market is a tourist attraction, in that tourist demand affects the code of utility of the market. Therefore, use-value is the equivalence of exchange-value, which does not relate to objects or subjects. Rowing boats and the opening times are fabricated cultural codes of utility in the market. Exchange-value, as well as codifiable utility, leads to what Baudrillard calls 'fetishism of use-value', which is needs and desire for the code of utility. This is pertinent to tourist expectation rather than intrinsic utility.

The fetishism of code: tourist-orientated change

Referring back to Baudrillard, 'the code' refers to the code of utility, or the status of utility. He states that people's needs are socially constructed, and this leads to 'the fetishism of use-value' (Baudrillard 1981, p. 135). Economic exchangeability does not only eclipse use-value but also leads to fetishism. The fetishism of code occurs after economic exchange-value has come into play. Local people fetishise the codes of the tourist-orientated floating markets.

According to the data, the fetishism of code means that the idea of the places meets tourist expectations.

As stated previously, tourist arrivals and road construction brought about the wish to re-establish Damnoen Saduak Floating Market, while the idea of nostalgia, along with tourism, recreates Pattaya Floating Market as a tourist attraction. The construction of the floating markets was about passion for tourist-orientated codes, which means the idea of the local floating market was introduced by flows of tourism. The reinvention of the floating markets requires that it meets tourist expectations. For Damnoen Saduak Floating Market, workers said it had changed from being part of a local way of life, to being a 'tourist-orientated place'.

> It used to be a fruit market where traders brought produce from their own fruit orchards to sell and exchange with one another.
>
> (Ms. Jin# n=26# female# Damnoen Saduak)

Having changed the purpose of the market, the place then became a tourist-orientated site. After seeing a significant increase in the number of tourists visiting, Damnoen Saduak Floating Market moved to the other side of the canal, next to the main road, and it was moved entirely for tourist-orientated purposes. The needs of local people, and the original purpose of the market, have been substituted with a tourist-orientated place, as the following interview data show.

ME: Was the floating market located here first?

INTERVIEWEE: No, it wasn't on this side, but the other side of the canal. The market was moved here because cars could only access this side of the canals. The market moved to this side about 20 to 30 years ago. (Ms. Pam# n=21# female# Damnoen Saduak)

Having been relocated, other changes occurred in the floating market. As interviewee no.7 said, 'The floating market is privately run by the different owners of boat services, and there are about ten boat services inside and outside the market' (Mr. Yingyong# n=25# male# Damnoen Saduak). Apart from the relocation and private boat services, there have been other tourist-orientated changes, namely, a few boat vendors, more tourist boats, motorboats, tourist-orientated careers, a better economy and income, a reduction in boat transportation, an increase in car transportation and extended waterways. For example:

> I stopped driving boats because of road transportation [networks] that now link to other areas in the city. Fewer tourists came to the market by boat. In the past, there was only one boat service. Now, there are many boat services to take tourists in and around the market.
>
> (Mr. Pete# n=19# male# Damnoen Saduak)

Those changes made the floating market become tourist-orientated spot. The place does not depend on the needs of local people or the purpose of the original floating market. The enthusiasm for reviving Damnoen Saduak Floating Market is regulated by the code of tourism, such as boat services for tourists.

Unlike Damnoen Saduak Floating Market, Pattaya Floating Market did not change from being part of the local way of life to a tourist place; rather, it appears to have been tourist orientated since the very beginning, and thus is inevitably subject to economic exchange-value and the code of tourism. The code demonstrated here is an idea of a floating market that accords with tourist expectations, whereby the place may offer a differentiated experience for tourists. For Thai tourists, their experience is differentiated from the outset with signage in Thai reading 'We are Thai, free entry'. Interviewees said they wanted Thai tourists to see traditional Thai culture from historical times, which cannot be found elsewhere.

Similarly, Cohen regards Pattaya Floating Market as an 'innovative new floating market that is themed to present aspects of Old Siam, or Thailand, in the architecture, or decor, albeit seen in business enterprises established by private entrepreneurs and planned as all-inclusive projects' (Cohen 2016, pp. 74–75). For Thai tourists, the code of nostalgia helps establish the place as a tourist site. Additionally, there are other significant tourist-orientated changes, as seen in the following:

ME: What has been a significant change in the market?

INTERVIEWEE: Well, we didn't call it change, as the concept of the place was the same, but we called it 'development', a constant development. We had old and new customers, old and new shops. We expanded the market and created new things that better fitted in the market. So, this was development rather than change. (Mr. Brad# n=10# male# Pattaya)

Pattaya Floating Market has seen expansion and experienced construction phases 2 and 3. The development of the market might refer to 'a good change'. The expansion of the floating market also meant lots of shops, more tourists, more traders, bigger tourist attractions and better tourist services. Another important tourist-orientated change was the construction of photographic backdrops.

ME: How long have you been working in the market?

INTERVIEWEE: About one and a half years.

ME: From the time you started working here until now [April 2015], what has been the most significant change?

INTERVIEWEE: In order to work in the floating market, I graduated with my first degree, in Communication Arts, from a university in Bangkok. While I was at university, I joined a drama club and I worked backstage. When I first came to the market, the market had no photography spot, or backdrop. Social media is important. Tourists visiting a place always take photos with lovely backdrops that they want to share on Facebook. So, I initiated the creation of backdrops and we received good feedback from tourists. They enjoyed taking photos and sharing them on Facebook, and this was free advertising for the market that encouraged tourists' friends and friends of friends to visit the market. (Ms. Petch# n=6# female# Pattaya)

From the interview data, tourist-orientated changes in Pattaya Floating Market, including the expansion of the market, the backdrops and more besides, do not relate to the physical place, which used to be a natural swamp, or to the subjects, or the workers who are employed in the market. Instead, the expansion of the market, as well as the backdrops, represents the drive for codes in a tourist-orientated place.

Such changes are not free from the influence of global flows. Tourist-orientated codes regulate workers' skills and help them establish the floating market. They also affect the purpose of the floating market, for example, the creation of picturesque backdrops changes the codes of tourist-orientated places, the organisation of the relationship between the objects in the places and the relationship between workers and tourists. Backdrops present the way the market should be framed or gazed upon. Tourists know what to do; they enjoy taking photos, while workers encourage them to share the photos on Facebook. The thirst for the codes of tourist-orientated places constitutes the desire of people and continually maintains the spread of tourism. As Baudrillard states, fetishism closely relates to the generalisation of exchange-value, whereby objects become commutable with sign-value. With the fetishism of tourist-orientated codes, Damnoen Saduak and Pattaya Floating Markets saw the transformation of their sign-value.

The play of representations

Referring back to Chapter 4, the generalisation of exchange-value facilitates sign-value, meaning the production of commodities is accompanied by signification. As Baudrillard states, sign-value takes the forms of exchange-value and use-value, whereby exchange-value can function as 'discourse of communication', or in this case, a cultural message for tourists, while use-value is only decoded as sign. So, what forms of signifier and signified does the circulation of value produce? We can discover this from the following data.

Analogy

The below photograph illustrates its current incarnation. In the context of Damnoen Saduak Floating Market, the analogy refers to 'the old market' and 'the new market'. Despite moving to the other side of the canal, Damnoen Saduak Floating Market sells itself as the original. What happened before that? A worker compares the traditional floating market with the current Damnoen Saduak Floating Market below.

> More than 30 years ago [1985–1986], there was the old, traditional and original floating market, named Khlong Lud Pee Floating Market or Lao Tak Lak Floating Market [a Chinese name], which was located on another side of the canals and run by the local municipality. We called it 'the old market' and it used to be a local trading centre, selling produce from local

Figure 5.1 Damnoen Saduak Floating Market

Source: Water Lim.

Note: Please visit www.youtube.com/watch?v=xWNcvtGEeY8&feature=youtu.be to see a full video of the original floating market in 1970, when it was called Khlong Lud Pee Floating Market.

fruit orchards. King Rama V allocated this land to Chinese immigrants. Local culture was thus a mixture of Chinese and Thai culture.

(Mr. Yingsak# n=30# male# Damnoen Saduak)

The current Damnoen Saduak Floating Market is not the original market; it replaced the old and original floating market, Khlong Lud Pee Floating Market. The old market, which had existed for more than 100 years, disappeared because of the relocation. Thus, the relocation of the market caused the code of utility to substitute its objective utility. The code of utility is dependent upon tourist arrivals. The use-value of the current Damnoen Saduak Floating Market is an effect of exchange-value. The existence of the floating market is a signifier, and the original place is a signified.

Having been moved to the other side of the canal, the old floating market disappeared. The current floating market has been established and privately owned by different boat-service owners but has been functioning as an original floating market. However, for the past 10 years, the local municipality has revived 'the old market' on Lud Pee Canal in order to preserve and restore local traditional culture.

ME: Do you mean there are two floating markets at the moment?

INTERVIEWEE: Yes, Damnoen Saduak Floating Market [the current market] was the first floating market of Thailand to be widely popular among tourists. But, Khlong Lud Pee, or Lao Tak Lak Floating Market, is called 'the old market'. The floating market used to be located on the Lud Pee Canal, then moved to the Damnoen Saduak Canal, for it was much more convenient for car trans-portation. Now, the municipality is reviving the old floating market.

ME: Now?

INTERVIEWEE: Yes, only some tourists visit the old market. Attractive spots are the Big Buddha of Rad Charoentum Temple, rowing boats and the traditional Thai way of life. It's open daily. If tourists came here, they would see a natural way of life.

ME: Are there several shops in the old market?

INTERVIEWEE: Well, some shops, but not as many as in Damnoen Saduak Floating Market.

ME: How long have you been reviving the old market?

INTERVIEWEE: For a long time, about 10 years. The anniversary of Damnoen Saduak Floating Market was held in the old market.

(Ms. Nat# n=24# female# Damnoen Saduak)

Also, the old market is run by the local municipality, but is not that popular with tourists. There's one coffee shop and one noodle boat over there. Group tours don't come to the old market as it is not close to the main road. Most vendors go to the new market.

(Ms. Wang# n=22# female# Damnoen Saduak)

From the interview data, the economic exchange-value of tourism makes the floating market (signifier) become a tourist attraction to display the local way of life (the code of utility), with the place claiming to be the original (signified). Whereas the revived old market that is useful for displaying and preserving the natural way of life (use-value), becomes merely the old market (signified). The old market that used to be the original water trading centre does not appear to be the original, as the existence of the current Damnoen Saduak Floating Market does not allow the other one to do so. In other words, Damnoen Saduak Floating Market is the analogy of the old revived floating market, with the current market selling itself as being original. Additionally, its code of utility, or use-value that is abstract, is only the effect of the economic exchange-value, or signifier. The old market is reduced to being an alibi of the current Damnoen Saduak Floating Market. The old floating market and the current Damnoen Saduak Floating Market involve both the logic of the commodity and the logic of sign.

To generalise exchange-value, it functions as a form of communication, whereby Damnoen Saduak Floating Market represents the original way of life. Damnoen Saduak Floating Market is a tourist attraction comprising a combination of signs, including the canal, boat transportation, boat service, wooden houses, floating vendors, rowing boats, shops and more besides. The exchange-value and signifier have become the legitimisation of utilities of those objects.

Regarding the revived old market, it was re-established by the local municipality to preserve local traditions and the culture of the past. The relation of exchange-value with use-value is equivalent to the relation of signifier with the signified, for the revived old market does not serve its objective function. Furthermore, the old market is a substitute for the current Damnoen Saduak Floating Market. Tourist arrivals caused the old market to disappear, as it did not fit into the context of tourism. The objective utility of the old floating market is abstract and renders the place exchangeable with tourist-orientated signs in accordance with tourism. Since the revived old market has lost its original status to the current floating market, it is subject to another set of tourist-orientated signs, or 'the discourse of communication' (exchange-value), such as one coffee shop, a rowing boat, a noodle boat, a natural way of life and the like, so as to rationalise the utility of the market.

The signifier and signified of the revived old market turn out to accord with the current Damnoen Saduak Floating Market and tourism. In this way, the circulation of use-value and exchange-value, and of signifier and signified, affects the emergence of the old and current floating markets as tourist attractions, with the objective utility of the floating markets being equivalent to convertible signs that only produce its rationalised social usage. In contrast to Damnoen Saduak Floating Market, Pattaya Floating Market is not an analogy of an old floating market; instead, it is an inherent copy. The differentiation between Pattaya Floating Market and Damnoen Saduak Floating Market will be elaborated on in the next section.

Manipulating signs

Prior to elaborating on interview data, it needs to be stressed that the logic of the commodity is equivalent to the logic of the sign. Instead of using the word 'analogy', the term 'manipulating signs' will be employed to show how Pattaya Floating Market engages the play of representation, where the place becomes partially connected to, and disconnected from, the original floating market. Signs that show a disconnection from original floating markets will be elaborated in Chapters 7 and 8.

Figure 5.2 below shows the present-day Pattaya Floating Market. It is fairly new, having been established in 2008. But paradoxically, it presents a well-organised and well-displayed ancient Thai culture. Coded data, derived from interviews

Figure 5.2 Pattaya Floating Market
Source: Horiuchi.

with workers in Pattaya Floating Market, are categorised into two types: connection to the original floating market; and disconnection from the floating market. Pattaya Floating Market needs signs to become a floating market, including boat vendors, floating shops, waterways, the ambience of water trading, riverbanks, piers, wooden houses, stalls on wooden paths, cooking on small rowing boats and boat rides. These sign objects take the form of the floating market and affect the emergence of the place as tourist attraction. However, some informants regarded the market as different from the original floating markets, as shown subsequently.

> Well, we have an amphibious boat here that tourists could have a ride on. We were located in Pattaya city, which was one of the most famous cities for tourists.
>
> (Mr. Chris# n=2# male# Pattaya)

Amphibious boats and the location are sign objects that disconnect Pattaya Floating Market from original floating markets. The most significant thing is 'being a copy', which means a constructed place intrinsically becomes a tourist attraction from the very beginning. The market is sold as a commodity to tourists, and its use-value is only an effect of exchange-value. Referring back to Baudrillard, the logic of the commodity thus anchors it in the logic of the sign.

The floating market was constructed to welcome tourist arrivals to famous Pattaya city. As a tourist attraction, Pattaya Floating Market is subject to exchange-value that functions as economic exchangeability and communication exchangeability, which is, in turn, interchangeable with other signs and signifiers. Sign-value comes into play, and it eclipses exchange-value and use-value. Thus, use-value becomes decoded, or signified; for instance, boat vendors and waterways are reduced to being an analogy of the original floating market.

Use-value and the signified become the alibis of economic exchange-value and signifier, respectively. Or rather, the former is created in accordance with the latter. The boat vendors, waterways, ambience, floating shops and more besides are signs that show connection to the original floating market, whereas the copy of that place, with amphibious boats, an attractive location, regional Thai performances and popularity as a film location are convertible signs that represent a disconnection from original floating markets. With commutable signs that connect to and disconnect from floating markets, Pattaya Floating Market marks itself as a differentiated tourist attraction.

Having elaborated on the circulation of value and signs, we can see how sign-value appears to function as the exchange-value and use-value of Damnoen Saduak and Pattaya Floating Markets. It is important now to direct our attention to tourists in terms of their perception of the floating markets, which enables us to understand how signs communicate with tourists and results in the two floating markets appearing on the tourist stage.

Tourist perceptions

To study tourists who have been to Damnoen Saduak and Pattaya Floating Markets, I conducted documentary research, selecting the 30 most recent comments for each market that tourists posted on TripAdvisor from 4 June 2015 to 20 June 2015. They were from tourists who had been part of group tours and independent travellers. Data obtained from TripAdvisor suggest that tourists are able to go with the flow. With the circulation of value, along with the play of representation, most tourists find the two floating markets acceptable.

Being acceptable for tourists means that the markets are worth visiting. At Damnoen Saduak Floating Market, tourists saw it as the original. Based on the comments, being an acceptable experience is divided into three groups. First, the market was acceptable for them because it appeared to be the original place:

> It was the original floating market, although it did seem to be a bit organised.
>
> (comment no.7# Damnoen Saduak)

Second, the market was an acceptable place, in that they could enjoy things in the market, such as buying food and taking a boat ride:

I saw tourists having fun with buying food and other items.

(comment no.4# Damnoen Saduak)

It was a nice experience to be on a boat and have a meal on a boat.

(comment no.17# Damnoen Saduak)

Third, although the market was a construct for tourists, it was worth a visit. For example,

It was really not a typical market anymore, it was more a tourist spot, but it was still worth the visit.

(comment no.22# Damnoen Saduak)

It was worth seeing and bargaining.

(comment no.5# Damnoen Saduak)

It was a tourist trap, yet you should visit once for the sake of saying been there and done that.

(comment no.13# Damnoen Saduak)

Going for the experience.

(comment no.19# Damnoen Saduak)

At this point, what affects tourist perceptions of Damnoen Saduak Floating Market is not the objective utility but rather the sign-value. The exchange-value of Damnoen Saduak Floating Market, or 'discourse of communication', determines the code of utility or signified, for instance, being acceptable means that the place is either original, or worth a visit for the sake of saying 'been there', while those meanings (use-value) are rational decoding. Sign-value takes the form of exchange-value and use-value, and it generalises exchange-value and rationalises use-value.

In relation to Pattaya Floating Market, being an acceptable place for tourists revealed what they enjoyed in the market. The following comments are examples.

There were eight boats in my hour visit, and two boats played some lovely music. The market was nice with various food and souvenir options.

(comment no.8# Pattaya)

There were lots to do and to explore, and it offered a good family experience.

(comment no.21# Pattaya)

The things that made Pattaya Floating Market acceptable for tourists were the boats, music, activity, family experience, food and souvenirs. As with Damnoen Saduak Floating Market, visiting the floating market was also a must-do activity for tourists.

It was nice to go to say you have been there.

(comment no.8# Pattaya)

According to the comments on TripAdvisor, Pattaya Floating Market is an acceptable place for tourists, as there are many things in the market to be enjoyed. Some of the contributors to the site stated that they had visited the place for the sake of saying 'been there'. An attempt to construct an acceptable place for tourists bolsters the exchange-value of the floating market so that the market meets tourist expectations, and sign exchange-value as 'the discourse of communication' helps legitimise use-value. For instance, if tourists see some boats during their visit, they find the market acceptable.

However, some tourists re-read signs of the floating markets differently from the cultural connotations attributed by the markets. From the data, some tourists perceive the two markets as a 'must-do' activity, meaning that they just follow the codes and norms of holidays without paying attention to the unique cultural messages of each market. In Damnoen Saduak and Pattaya Floating Markets, signs of the original market and of traditional culture may not be that important for tourists, because they just want to enjoy seeing a market. The markets are acceptable to them because they are enjoyable places. Although Baudrillard's theory enables us to see how sign-value takes the forms of use-value and exchange-value, his theory might oversimplify issues of value and code.

Theoretical discussions

The conception of globalised tourism

With circulation of value and sign, tourism in the floating markets becomes global, for the locations involve the movement of people, flows of culture and the movement of capital. But the term 'global tourism' cannot tell us how global flows affect tourism in a local place. As stated in Chapter 4, globalised tourism refers to the effect of global flows on tourism in a local place where the difference between contrived culture for tourists and the local culture is effaced. In this chapter, I will show that what is globalised is the exchangeability of each floating market with money and cultural signs. In this manner, tourism in the floating markets that is inherently local becomes globalised rather than global, since their use-value becomes exchangeable with other cultural signs.

This makes the utilities of the revived traditional floating market (Damnoen Saduak) and of the artificial floating market (Pattaya) replaceable. Damnoen Saduak and Pattaya Floating Markets have become tourist attractions, and the emergence of the places is subject to economic exchange-value induced by global flows. This causes the use-value of the floating markets to be recreated in accordance with tourist demand. This may be referred back to Baudrillard's hyperculture. The code of utility introduced by the global replaces the real use-value of the floating markets, for example, the sign-value of boat services in the floating markets eclipses the use-value of boats for transportation. The distinction between use-value of an object/place and the code of utility for tourist purposes is eroded. Although Baudrillard's idea enables me to develop the concept of globalised tourism, his work has some limitations in understanding use-value and 'the code'.

The limitations of Baudrillard's theory

Use-value has no autonomy at all (Baudrillard 1981, p. 139). This implies exchange-value and use-value have a causal relationship, whereby the former determines the latter. However, Baudrillard is overly pessimistic in denying that use-value has autonomy. In this way, Baudrillard's work still represents economic reductionism, through which he regards needs, desire and use-value to be socially constructed in accordance with economic exchangeability. Use-value, to some extent, is subject to economic exchangeability and communication exchangeability, or sign-value, in tourism, though it also relates to people's needs and desires. I would say use-value of the markets as well as people's needs can change anyway, depending on the current context. We do not expect the utility of places/objects to remain the same. It is impossible to say that use-value does not relate to personal satisfaction at all.

Kellner argues that we are able to specify what needs and use-values of various commodities serve our own purposes and self-defined needs, but, to at least some degree, one can generally determines one's needs, or create one's own use-values, and hence evaluate commodities in accordance with their uses for specific ends and projects (Kellner 1989, p. 38). In contrast to Baudrillard, Kellner regards use-value as subjective, whereby people can use commodities to satisfy self-defined needs. One's own use-value might be different from another's use-value; what is useful for one group of people might not satisfy a different group. In reference to the case studies, the floating markets are tourist attractions and they may satisfy local people's needs. Damnoen Saduak Floating Market was established after being moved to the other side of the canals, next to the main road in order to be convenient for tourists travelling to the market by car. The arrival of tourists has caused significant changes in the market, yet the code of utility induced by tourism may be internalised, which then becomes the local people's use of the market. Because of road construction, local workers travel to the floating market by car, then transfer to boat in order to act as floating vendors.

Their mode of transportation, along with staged culture, turns out to fulfil local people's needs, with them commuting to the floating market by car so as to avoid tourist boats on the canals. Commuting to the market by car takes less time than by boat. In this way, use-value appears to be the everyday culture of local people who are able to make use of the market to satisfy their needs. On the one hand, the utility of Damnoen Saduak Floating Market is dependent on the economic exchange-value in tourism, though on the other hand, this may become routine in people's everyday life so that that they can make use of it for different ends. In Pattaya Floating Market, tourist arrivals and economic exchange play a more important role in determining the code of utility than they do in Damnoen Saduak Floating Market. Since the place did not spontaneously occur, the construction of Pattaya Floating Market depends on the owner's motivation to preserve Thai culture. The utility of the place, in this way, is subjective.

Regarding tourists, the floating markets are an acceptable experience for them because of their cultural messages and sign-value, rather than the objective utility of the markets. For example, they perceive Damnoen Saduak Floating Market as original, and their perception is consonant with the cultural connotation created by the place. Or rather, the tourists just follow the norms and codes of holiday-ing in Thailand, whereby they view the two markets as must-do activities. How-ever, the utility of Damnoen Saduak and Pattaya Floating Markets for tourists may differ from that for local people. Tourists find these two markets acceptable as they can enjoy seeing things in the places rather than conforming to codes and holidays.

Tourists, in this way, are able to perform 'the second gaze' as suggested by MacCannell (2001). Referring back to MacCannell in Chapter 3, tourists know that a place is not original, instead is constructed, and they do not believe what they see. They perceive that something may be hidden behind it. In the case of the two markets, the data show some tourists do not perceive the places according to the cultural messages and signs of the floating markets. Instead, they observe through their own gaze, through which they view the floating markets as enjoyable.

Regarding Baudrillard, his work may have limitations in understanding sign-value, since it is reduced to be the effect of economy, whereby he states the logic of commodity is associated with the logic of signification. However, Böhme and Engels-Schwarzpaul (2016, p. 11) argue that the aesthetic, or stage-value, is an autonomous type of value, with further qualities being added in order to exchange a commodity's exchange-value, and the aesthetic economy linked with developed capitalism witnessing the relative increase of commodities that only have aesthetic value. Aesthetic quality makes economic exchange-value increase, and some commodities may be produced to serve only the purpose of atmosphere, such as using different materials to suit the preferences of different groups of people. In this manner, aesthetic value is dependent upon the actor, or producer, rather than the market. To further understand the production of stage-value, we may need to pay more attention to the actor in the production process.

Regarding the code, Baudrillard emphasises that the logic of commodities is associated with the logic of significations, but sign-value is undertheorised in his work. How these two are developed in the capitalist economy is left unclear. To better elaborate on the term 'signs', Böhme and Engels-Schwarzpaul assert that, in contemporary aesthetics, reference and understanding of signs are pos-sible only insofar as they are embedded in culture: signs are conventional (2016, p. 4). References of signs are based on culture and tradition. In the case of the floating markets, what becomes the code of utility and sign-value is the local way of life and the idea of nostalgia.

Furthermore, Baudrillard may overstate the predominance of the code over object and subject. To debate this point, Kellner contends, 'Baudrillard sees the code as an overarching regulative principle or system that determines the relative prestige or sign-value of commodities, yet it is not clear who establishes the code, or how it functions in specific cases' (Kellner 1989, p. 30). The problem is that Baudrillard uses the term 'the code' in a general sense that appears to be overarching the structures of the systems. In other words, the system of codes comes to govern both the subject and object. This is a one-way relationship between the code and society.

The system of codes may not intrinsically happen, as the code is a kind of language game. The system of codes, to some extent, depends on the relationship between subject and object. The code of an object affects the desire and needs of people, yet the subject simultaneously modifies it. Baudrillard does not elaborate on how the system of codes is constituted. It is thus hard to identify 'the code' in practical case studies. In the case of the floating markets, I suggest the places engage in interaction between the global and the local. There must be some sets of codes that are consonant with tourism, while there might be other sets of codes created by local people, or even pre-established by local culture. Locally produced codes of a traditional way of life and floating markets might be precedents for flows of tourism.

With the natural attributes of Damnoen Saduak Floating Market, the place becomes an original floating market (instead of the revived old market) and an acceptable place for tourists. Tourists are able to enjoy the place and even perceive it as must-see destination. Damnoen Saduak Floating Market appears to be original, because to some extent, it presents locally produced codes and signs of floating markets, including a local way of life, canals, boats, floating vendors and Thai ambience, while those sign objects happen to meet tourist expectations.

Pattaya Floating Market, however, is a constructed place, and a copy that displays locally constructed codes and sign objects that connect to traditional floating markets, namely, waterways, boats, vendors, banks and piers. But some codes show disconnection from a traditional floating market, such as different entrance signs for Thai and foreign tourists, the amphibious boat, its location, its existence as a contrived market and so on. On the one hand, these are locally produced sign-values, but on the other, they are created by sign-value for tourism. Locally produced signs may juxtapose with signs induced by tourism, especially the differentiation between the Thai-tourist entrance and foreign-tourist entrance. The sign reading in Thai 'We are Thai, free entry' shows that income from domestic tourism does not matter to the floating market. What they produce and offer in the market is not principally made for Thai tourists.

However, foreign tourists must pay an admission fee and therefore income from international tourism matters to the emergence of Pattaya Floating Market; cultural value along with an experience of a floating market and Thai culture are specifically created for foreign tourists, especially Chinese ones. This will be discussed further in the following chapters. In this way, Pattaya Floating Market can mediate flows of tourism, albeit in a contrived place. We should bear in mind that Damnoen Saduak and Pattaya Floating Markets have become tourist attractions due to both locally pre-established codes and tourist-orientated codes. Therefore, 'the code' cannot be treated as totality.

Conclusion

From the interview data, it can be seen that the globalisation and tourism involved in flows of capital, tourist arrivals, the economic system and unequal flows of cash, to some extent, foster the circulation of value and signs. It permits signs to take the forms of the floating markets, where signs function as both exchange-value and use-value. They are tourist attractions because of the circulation of value and signs. Despite the play of value and signs, most tourists find the two floating markets acceptable when they are able to go with the flow. For tourists, the floating markets are worth a visit.

Having seen in what ways these places are tourist attractions, it is now necessary to turn to the cultural contents of the floating markets.

References

Baudrillard, J. (1981). *For a Critique of the Political Economy of the Sign.* Trans. C. Levin. St. Louis, MO: Telos Press.

Böhme, G. and Engels-Schwarzpaul, T. (2016). Material Splendour. A Contribution to the Critique of Aesthetic Economy. In: G. Bohme (ed), *Atmospheric Architectures: The Aesthetics of Felt Spaces.* Trans. by T. Engels-Schwarzpaul. London: Bloomsbury, pp. 55–69.

Cohen, E. (2016). The Permutations of Thailand's 'Floating Markets'. *Asian Journal of Tourism Research*, 1(1), 59–98.

Kellner, D. (1989). *Jean Baudrillard: From Marxism to Postmodernism and Beyond.* Stanford, CA: Stanford University Press.

MacCannell, D. (2001). Tourist Agency. *Tourist Studies*, 1(1), 23–37.

Pongajarn, C., Van der Duim, R. and Peters, K. (2016). Floating Markets in Thailand: Same, Same, but Different. *Journal of Tourism and Cultural Change*, 16(2), 109–122.

6 A false dichotomy of globalisation and the play of differences

Introduction

With the circulation of signs, how does globalisation and tourism affect the cultural contents of the floating markets? This chapter focuses on the cultural contents of Damnoen Saduak and Pattaya Floating Markets, or the production and consumption of cultural value in the places. The cultural contents of the floating markets enable each place to differentiate itself from the other, and to attract tourists. This chapter examines whether there is any difference between the interpretations of Thai workers and those of tourists in regard to Thai culture. It also examines to what extent Ritzer's theory fits into a non-Western context of Thailand. Ritzer's theory may be an example of the whole strand of globalisation and he proposes that globalisation is dichotomised to give two categories of 'something' and 'nothing'.

However, this seems to be too simple a way to study the cultural contents of the floating markets, that is, Ritzer's theory appears to be a false dichotomy. Since the circulation of value and signs propels the floating markets into being tourist attractions, I suggest that there are no fixed criteria that separate distinctive cultural content from generic cultural content. I will suggest the cultural contents and cultural value of the two floating markets do not differ from each other significantly. In order to challenge Ritzer, Baudrillard's theory of 'the system of objects' will be employed. For Baudrillard, the cultural content of an object does not depend on its practical application, but on the relationship between the object and the subject, or the relationship between an object and its context.

The first section of this chapter presents interview data on workers and data analysis. Pattaya Floating Market involves the play of differences to a higher extent than Damnoen Saduak Floating Market, with the former turning out to be a series object. Second, data on tourists obtained from TripAdvisor will be presented so that we can understand tourist interpretation of the two floating markets with regard to Thai culture. The third section concerns theoretical discussions regarding the limitations of working with Ritzer's and Baudrillard's theories.

The definition of authenticity

Both Damnoen Saduak and Pattaya Floating Markets define themselves as authentic, and these places focus on creating value. The following interview data illustrate the signification of authenticity. How does each floating market define authenticity? Referring to the discussions in the Baudrillard chapter, interview data that contrast with Ritzer indicate there are no fixed criteria for differentiating distinctive cultural content from generic cultural content. Regardless of distinctive and indistinctive cultural content, a place can still become authentic. The cultural contents of the floating markets do not depend on practical application; therefore, their difference is not singular but abstract. Based on Baudrillard, an antique object is authentic when it relates to nostalgia for origin and the source of value. In this case, authenticity is anchored in the significations of time and of value. What is antique is thus authentic.

Damnoen Saduak Floating Market: originality

Damnoen Saduak Floating Market sees its cultural content as 'original'. Interviewees mentioned this floating market was natural, or it represented the genuine way of life of local people. The below exchange is an example.

ME: What makes Damnoen Saduak Floating Market more attractive than other markets?

INTERVIEWEE: Well, this market is original and genuine.

ME: OK! How would you tell tourists that this place is original or genuine?

INTERVIEWEE: This place is absolutely original and has existed for more than 100 years.

ME: What is original in the market?

INTERVIEWEE: Like those fruit, we didn't buy them from Pak Khlong Talat Flower Market [in Bangkok]. What is sold here was brought from local fruit orchards.

ME: Right! Why do tourists want to visit the place?

INTERVIEWEE: They want to see an old-fashioned market, which they couldn't find back home. This market is an old-fashioned place in Thailand. Water trading became a local tradition and a way of life. Tourists love to see things that are outdated and not modern. They can't find this kind of market in their home countries, where there are floating vendors or you can eat noodles on boats. Tourists like to see things that are opposite to their life back home. They don't like high technological stuff because they have it back home.

(Mr. Pong# n=20 # male# Damnoen Saduak)

'Original' refers to the signifying time that the market has existed, 100 years, and the nostalgia for origins, where objects in the market relate to the specific locality. What makes original content stand out is the away experience: the original floating market is different from what tourists experience in their home country. Damnoen Saduak Floating Market is an original floating market because it shows traces of the past and that becomes the source of value. To define cultural content as original, Damnoen Saduak Floating Market seems to invoke nostalgia for its origins; the old-fashioned place is re-created to signify time of its existence. In the meantime, the market derives authenticity from its source of value, such as locality, tradition, the way of life and its fruit farmers. The original and authentic content of the market is thus embedded in the relationship between the place and its subjects.

The source of value that makes Damnoen Saduak Floating Market more attractive to tourists than other places is its natural ambience, closeness to Bangkok, the daily market, convenience for travelling and its worldwide reputation.

ME: What makes Damnoen Saduak Floating Market famous?

INTERVIEWEE: The market has a natural ambience and the advantage of being close to Bangkok. When people think about going to a floating market, Damnoen Saduak Floating Market is the first place that comes to mind. Our vendors are local people who grow local produce to sell and exchange with others.

(Ms. Nat# n=24# female# Damnoen Saduak)

In this manner, the demand for authenticity is an obsession with the source of value that is anchored in the relationship between the object and subject. Although Damnoen Saduak Floating Market appears to be authentic, it is not in itself authentic, rather, the floating market functions as a sign of nostalgia, namely local tradition and way of life, and also as a sign of witness, as seen in its worldwide reputation. Damnoen Saduak Floating Market becomes an original place, and what makes the place authentic is not the market itself, or its practical application, but rather its association with the signification of time and the source of value. Since the cultural contents of the place are open to a combinatory system of sign, the place involves the play of differences.

Pattaya Floating Market: 'Thainess'

Unlike Damnoen Saduak Floating Market, 'Thainess' is the source of value that enables Pattaya Floating Market to become authentic. This confirms the findings of Pongajarn,Van der Duim and Peters (2016, p. 10), which suggest Pattaya Floating Market connects Pattaya with the rest of Thailand, rather than representing the locality of Pattaya. Despite being a copy, Pattaya Floating Market is constructed as a tourist-orientated place that preserves Thainess. The place can claim authenticity, and it attempts to beat a path back to its origins, or to a mother to whom it has never belonged. The floating market itself exists only in the present and never in a former time. Pongajarn et al. (2016, p. 10) also state that floating markets in Pattaya city were previously non-existent. Pattaya Floating Market becomes attractive to tourists because of the concept of Thainess. Interviewees see Thainess as important to the floating market, namely water trading in the past, water transportation and the old way of life.

ME: Was Pattaya Floating Market created to preserve Thainess?

INTERVIEWEE: Yes, the Thai way of life in the past referred to boat transportation [80%]. The owner really likes boats because he comes from Ayutthaya province [the old capital of Thailand]. We had, like, 40–50 boats here to offer boat-ride services to tourists. We are now using 30 boats. Water transportation, which was the Thai way of life in the past, caused the floating market to emerge. No matter whether local people were going to Bangkok, or Ayutthaya, boat was the main mode of transportation. There was no road, just forest, which was dangerous. Only the rich could travel on land, such as by elephant. But people normally used boats, cooked on boats, and stopped in different areas. People sold and exchanged what they had on boats, such as chilli and eggplants. This is why the floating market emerged. Our place really takes tourists back to old times.

(Mr. Sam# n=3# male# Pattaya)

Thainess, which refers to uniqueness and authenticity, is the cultural content of Pattaya Floating Market. Undoubtedly, the floating market itself does not inherently become authentic, authenticity is socially constructed. Thainess is embedded in nostalgia, which is a regression into the past. Thainess does not relate to practical application of the place, but rather the source of value signifying time. As Baudrillard states, an antique object is authentic. Pattaya Floating Market is unique, for the cultural content of Thainess relates to the moment of creation, or the birth, of the floating market. Thainess is the play of differences, which makes the cultural content of the market abstract. It is only with marginal differences that the status of authenticity can function.

Apart from signification of time, Thainess also refers to the source of value, which includes personal characteristics, namely hospitality, Thai greetings, Thai markets, Thai manners, Thai language, a smile and a warm welcome. In this way, Thainess makes the cultural content of the market distinctive. Thainess derives its meanings from the relationship between the place and subject. Mr. Liam clearly states how the word 'Thainess' was created in the following text.

INTERVIEWEE: You know! It is very easy to understand the word, but to explain it is a bit complicated, but I'll try. The word 'Thainess' first means to give support to everybody, showing smiling faces, giving them a warm welcome, having the instinct to take care of them, presenting your old style to them, being open-minded and so on.

ME: Um, the concept of Thainess is a bit abstract.

INTERVIEWEE: I created it on a big billboard on the motorway – 'Pattaya Floating Market, the Home of Exotic Culture and Charming Thainess'. This word was my creation. It was a long time before TAT [Tourism Authority of Thailand] used this! I was a bit surprised when I saw them using this word to promote Thailand, but it was not an easy time for the Thai tourism market then. You know TAT [called Tor Tor Tor in Thai] talks about 'Exploring Thainess'. But I had used this word already, a long time ago, before TAT created that phrase.

(Mr. Liam# n=4# male# Pattaya)

As a constructed place, it is necessary for Pattaya Floating Market to demand authenticity and the source of value, so as to invent cultural content. The floating market uses the word 'Thainess' in order to become a distinctive place. The demand for authenticity, along with the creation of Thainess, based on the data, is an obsession with certainty, such as origin, date, author and signature of a work. Thainess created by the market appears to be the signature of the floating market.

Therefore, signification of time and the source of value make the floating market antique and authentic, and the demand for value permits the place to exist in the present. Although Damnoen Saduak and Pattaya Floating Markets introduce the different concepts of originality and Thainess, the places are marginally different from each other, since the cultural contents of the markets do not depend on their practical application, but rather significations of time and value. Establishing the source of value does not only involve fixation on certainty, but also on searching for others, which will be presented now.

Contested authenticity and searching for authenticity

In this section, authenticity refers to the presence of others. Damnoen Saudak and Pattaya Floating Markets claim to be authentic because of the emergence of the other. In this case, contested authenticity means 'what I do is better than what others do'. Damnoen Saduak and Pattaya Floating Markets are endowed with a source of value, with which they sometimes contest each other. The emergence of the other enables each floating market to become authentic. For Damnoen Saduak Floating Market, the original cultural content of the place is opposed to that of a constructed market. A constructed floating market is defined as follows.

> A constructed floating market hires people to sell stuff to create an image of a floating market and gain income. They tell tourists that their market is a local way of life, but it is not. They try to make the place look like a floating market to fool tourists. They just dug a canal, but it is not a floating market, as seen with Pattaya. They dug a beautiful canal and let their land to earn an income. It is like that. But those are not genuine markets. The genuine Damnoen Saduak Floating Market was local trading for local people, which took a very long time for local people to gather together and sell stuff. But those constructed markets create an image of trading. It is not trading, just exploitation!
>
> (Mr. Pong# n=20# male# Damnoen Saduak)

The demand for authenticity does not inherently occur in the market, rather it is contested in other places. The floating market pits its cultural content against that of artificial floating markets, so as to draw a contrast between itself and others. Another example follows.

> Here, we didn't dig a canal like the one called Ayothaya Floating Market. This is the real Damnoen Saduak Canal, and the Damnoen Saduak community

lived by the canals. We didn't construct the canal to build shops and stalls in the markets like Hua Hin Floating Market, or Sam Phan Nam Floating Market in Thai [located in Hua Hin city, famous for beautiful beaches]. Our Damnoen Saduak Floating Market is a natural place [I think she meant genuine[1]]. Some tourists criticise our place, but this doesn't stop other tourists visiting here. Damnoen Saduak Floating Market is linked with other small canals. We didn't make up the canals, they were ordered to be built in the reign of King Rama IV, and later finished in the reign of King Rama V. It was named Damnoen Saduak because the canal connected to other small canals, making water transportation much more convenient.

(Ms. Pam# n=21# female# Damnoen Saduak)

The status of authenticity/being authentic derives from the emergence of other floating markets, especially Pattaya and Hua Hin Floating Markets. Damnoen Saduak Floating Market uses other artificial floating markets to legitimise its authenticity. The original and genuine cultural contents of the market become distinctive only when they are cultural contents as opposed to other artificial floating markets.

Regarding Pattaya Floating Market, being a copy does not preclude the place from engaging in contested authenticity – 'I can be better than you, despite being a constructed floating market'.

ME: The place is not authentic, right?

INTERVIEWEE: Not authentic, no! What we did here is man-made. We didn't do a traditional and old floating market, but we had advantages. We did man-made, so we could follow our own style. You could plan everything in advance. But a historical one ... for example, if you go to a traditional one like Damnoen Saduak, you have to get up early in the morning, like 6 or 7, or 8 o'clock, and everything disappears at noon. It is not that convenient, especially for tourists, because they like to sleep. In the evening, they go to a bar to have a drink, go to bed late and don't want to get up that early. So that [making our opening times later] has made our floating market successful.

ME: I have seen comments on some websites, like TripAdvisor, like this – 'This place is a replica of a real floating market and this market was made up for tourists, but the place was not usual, so is not to be missed'. Do you agree or disagree with that?

INTERVIEWEE: Of course, we needed to see the commercial side of the area. It wasn't only about the floating market, but also the need to create something special. The area is nice. We have a floating market. Besides, at this place you're able to relax, or walk, not being chased by noisy motorbikes. So it's worth coming here, and it's also nice to get a glimpse of the atmosphere.

(Mr. Liam# n=4 # male# Pattaya)

Pattaya Floating Market thus makes its cultural content more unique by contesting that of traditional floating markets. For example, tourists do not need to get up early to visit Pattaya Floating Market, and it is a place where people can relax and walk comfortably. Some interviewees also attempted to draw a contrast between a copy and an original floating market.

INTERVIEWEE: Pattaya Floating Market offers a different ambience, so you can't compare it to that sort of market [original]. Here's a tourist attraction, but those markets were everyday life. If tourists visit those places, they can see the way of life of local Thai fruit farmers. But our market is tourist-orientated.

ME: What makes this market unique?

INTERVIEWEE: Well ... a variety of products and many groups of tourists, but in these markets [original], you can find only local products for daily life use. Our market attracts foreign tourists to visit, so we offer various types of product.

(Mr. Frank# n=15# male# Pattaya)

Being a tourist-orientated floating market is different from being an original floating market. Pattaya Floating Market is not an original place, and it provides a different ambience for tourists. The status of authenticity depends on the presence of other markets and the emergence of a traditional floating market turns out to be a source of value for Pattaya Floating Market.

Pattaya Floating Market was constructed and continually expanded. Some tourists have come here and said this was not the market they wanted to visit. We asked them why they wanted to visit markets like Damnoen Saduak and Amphawa. Our floating market is made up, while those markets have natural canals. It is different. If they go to those places, they could see natural ambience, such as canals, fruit orchards and so on. But we don't have those things here. What we have are shops. In those places, tourists can take a boat trip outside the market, experience local life and see fresh ingredients from orchards, like coconuts. But they can't see those kinds of things here. Our market had the opportunity to be situated in a better location. We can't compare to them because they are original.

(Mr. Kong# n=16# male# Pattaya)

The place is more distinctive than the original one in terms of the variety of products, different ambience and its better location. That cultural content only appears to be authentic when Pattaya Floating Market contests the original floating markets. Therefore, similar to Damnoen Saduak Floating Market, Pattaya Floating Market can also use the presence of the 'other' in the legitimisation of its authenticity. We cannot say Damnoen Saduak Floating Market is more distinctive than Pattaya Floating Market or vice versa. There are no fixed criteria to differentiate authentic culture from generic culture. This is because authenticity does not depend on practical application of the markets. Instead, it is dependent on the source of value that is the presence of the other. Pattaya Floating Market derives its authenticity from the emergence of the traditional floating market, whereas Damnoen Saduak Floating Market becomes authentic only after construction, and after other artificial floating markets have appeared. If there is only one floating market, and the difference is singular, the status of authenticity may not be that important. Apart from the definition of authenticity, what else is authentic in the floating markets?

Authentic products: the quest for an alibi

Authenticity is not about separating distinctive cultural content from indistinctive cultural content as Ritzer proposes. Ritzer says the former is embedded in the dimension of locality, while the latter is exposed to the global. If this were the case, then authenticity would seem to become polarised in regard to local culture and tourist-orientated culture. However, the interview data show that authenticity can be found in both distinctive and generic cultural contents. In contrast to Ritzer, Baudrillard (1996, p. 81) suggests, 'The quest for authenticity (being-founded-on-itself) is very precisely a quest for an alibi (being-elsewhere).' For Baudrillard, a quest for an alibi is the co-existence of antithetical objects, namely the mythological object and the functional object. The mythological object derives social usage from the existence of the functional object in the same context, whereas the functional object attains cultural value from the co-presence of the mythological object. Each search for an alibi lies in the other, and co-exists in a complementary way. In relation to the floating markets, the functional markets that serve tourist purposes need to look for alibis, or mythological objects, to fulfil the status of authenticity.

Authentic cultural contents are not objectively different. On the condition that the markets are functionally different, they would not search for authenticity and value; authenticity is therefore the play of differences. Functional and mythological objects in the floating markets refer to a variety of products that are assigned some purpose, or assigned cultural value. Interviewees in both Damnoen Saduak and Pattaya Floating Markets view their products as unique, and as items that distinguish one market from the other. In Damnoen Saduak Floating Market, products that are associated with authenticity are locally grown fruit and crops, along with souvenir items, as seen in the following interview data.

ME: Did you sell these souvenirs from the beginning?
INTERVIEWEE: At the beginning, my mum sold fruit, which we brought from our orchards. At first, we didn't sell tourist souvenir clothes.
ME: [Pointing to a mango.] Are these from your orchard?
INTERVIEWEE: No, we bought them. We have bananas and coconuts in our orchard, but we already cut down our mango trees. Before the floating market moved to this side, my mum and I rowed a boat to sell fruit in the old market [Khlong Lud Pee Floating Market]. About 20 years ago, this area of the current Damnoen Saduak Floating Market used to be filled with local vendors selling watermelon, garlic and onions.

ME: Selling watermelon here?

INTERVIEWEE: Yes, vendors sold garlic, pineapple and watermelon, and we didn't sell these clothes at all.

ME: Why did you change to sell clothes?

INTERVIEWEE: Since road transportation enables traders and intermediaries to access local orchards, they can easily bring produce to the other markets in the city. Local people don't come to this area to buy those crops, and we can't sell them. We decided to sell clothes instead, for clothes don't go rotten like fruit. What we sell now depended on a change in the environment. Intermediaries now buy fruit and crops directly from orchards. They don't need to travel to the floating market to buy produce.

(Ms. Pam# n=21# female# Damnoen Saduak)

Traders don't buy produce directly from orchards, yet there are some traders [intermediaries] who buy fruit and crops from orchards to sell to other vendors. Then those vendors offer the produce to tourists. In the past, local fruit farmers came directly from their homes to sell fruit and crops, but now vendors buy produce from intermediaries. They don't buy produce directly from orchards, as one orchard might grow a kind of fruit that is not convenient. Vendors go to another market in the city called Sri Muang Market to buy produce from fruit farmers, or get them from intermediaries. They get in their car, go to the floating market and arrange produce in the boat to perform as floating vendors. But if it's a boat vendor who offers only one product on a boat, such as guava, he or she might be a fruit farmer who has come directly from their orchard.

(Mr. Wong# n=23# # male# Damnoen Saduak)

Based on the interview data, although the arrival of tourists, along with road construction, has caused a change in product distribution, it does not mean local produce stops functioning in the floating market. Now the fruit that is being sold in the market is not brought from vendors' own local orchards, but by vendors who buy it from other intermediaries. In terms of meaning, fruit and crops signify origin and signature of a work, which means locally grown produce by fruit farmers. Damnoen Saduak Floating Market was a place selling local fruit and crops and became a place of local trading. The existence of a fruit market is the point of creation and the source of value.

Local fruit and crops that were once functional objects in Damnoen Saduak Floating Market are mythological objects, with vendors nowadays buying fruit and crops from intermediaries and arranging them on boats to sell to tourists. Local fruit and crops have maximal meaning that relates to the origin, but they have minimal function when assigned to serve some purpose to ensure that have a reason to be in the context of tourism. Local fruit and crops, or mythological objects, appear to be a cultural performance for tourists. The quest for authenticity is not found in local produce itself. This is because to be authentic, an object must be used. Local produce needs to search for an alibi, which is the co-presence of a functional object. So, having become one of the most famous tourist spots, which types of products function in Damnoen Saduak Floating Market? To respond to tourist demand, the floating market offers a variety of souvenirs, as noted below.

> The floating market used to offer only local produce, but now most vendors sell souvenirs. What was sold here has totally changed. They sell souvenirs on boats, though some are locally produced.
>
> > (Ms. Wang# n=22# female# Damnoen Saduak)

> In the past, local vendors sold fruit and crops that were grown in their orchards and came to the floating market to exchange them with others. But now, what is being sold is brought from other places and this makes our floating market look like other floating markets, especially Pattaya.
>
> > (Ms. Nat# n=24# female# Damnoen Saduak)

A souvenir is a functional object that has a maximal function, for its existence is associated with the context of tourism, or a souvenir is used to respond to tourist purposes. On the other hand, it has minimal meaning, whereby it possibly does not extend beyond the realm of tourism. In order to become authentic, the functional object (souvenir) has to search for an alibi that has cultural value, whereas the mythological object (fruit and crops) has to look for an alibi that has function. Therefore, the functional object (souvenir) co-presents with the mythological object (locally grown fruit and crops).

In contrast to Damnoen Saduak Floating Market, Pattaya Floating Market might be inauthentic because it does not have a function outside its performance for tourists. The fact that Pattaya city has beautiful beaches and islands does not relate to any traditional floating market. However, it might not be as simple as that. Workers in Pattaya Floating Market say, 'The place has more advantages than a traditional floating market, namely different ambience, location, various souvenirs and opening times'. In this way, Pattaya Floating Market is a functional place that is a tourist-orientated market where local vendors sell products to tourists. Unlike Damnoen Saduak Floating Market, each product that is sold in Pattaya Floating Market can be split into those that have functional and those that have mythological attributes. One interviewee mentioned how regional and OTOP products marked the place out as distinctive.

What is sold in Pattaya Floating Market becomes authentic, since the items that are sold there are carefully selected by the market. Interviewees say the market's department of product design has the responsibility of recruiting traders, choosing products to fit with the conception of Thainess and choosing the location for each product. Different products are sold in different zones of the market. The following interview data shows this.

ME: Do most shops sell identical items?
INTERVIEWEE: Not that similar! The products are different in each regional zone. In the Southern zone, vendors sell silverware, weaving products, and in the Northern zone they sell wooden items.

> > (Mr. Sam# n=3# male# Pattaya)

Apart from regional products, OTOP[2] products are offered at Pattaya Floating Market.

INTERVIEWEE: As a constructed, or man-made, market we can follow our own style, the idea being to promote OTOP products. You know OTOP, right?

ME: Yeah, OTOP.

INTERVIEWEE: OTOP stands for One Tambon [sub-district] One Product, and the idea initially came from Japan.

ME: Oh, Japan!

INTERVIEWEE: It was adopted in Thailand under the patronage of the royal family. Let's say they wanted to give a chance for people in rural areas to use materials, whatever they have, to create a product. In the floating market, you have the opportunity to find OTOP products in our shops. Imagine you are travelling, most people need to bring souvenirs back home to their beloved ones, or family, right? Imagine you walk along busy roads in Bangkok or Phuket! So our market is a good place for hunting for and buying souvenirs. Well, when I say souvenirs, I don't mean souvenirs in the traditional way, as in the kind you put on a sideboard, dust them and take good care of them. What I mean is a souvenir that is really worth using, like handmade soap [no chemicals]. When you come to our place, you are able to find designed products and unique items.

(Mr. Liam# n=4# male# Damnoen Saduak)

Thus, in the constructed and tourist-orientated floating market, a souvenir appears to be a functional object because the items are tourist-orientated. Tourists might want to buy souvenirs for their family and to remember visiting the place. As interviewees stated, souvenirs sold in Pattaya Floating Market are not traditional, but rather souvenirs for everyday use. Thus, souvenirs that are sold in the floating market do not only have a functional attribute, but also a mythological attribute. They are used to serve a tourist purpose, while they derive sign-value from the reference to regional Thai culture. They show a regression to origin and to the source of value. The status of authenticity of OTOP products does not only refer to the source of value in Thai culture, but also local adaptation of Japanese culture.

As the informant stated, the idea of OTOP originally came from Japan. The idea of OTOP has been internalised within local Thai culture and has become the source of value of Thai products. Looking back at Baudrillard's theory, the different terms of functional attribute and mythological attribute can co-exist with their counterpart in a complementary fashion. Functional and mythological attributes can co-present in one product, which enables the product to be authentic. For example, silverware that is manufactured in the south of Thailand has the signification of value (the place of creation), and is also used to serve the tourist trade (souvenir).

Moreover, another well-known souvenir is 'yellow oil',[3] which is a product created by the market (the market's product), and is one of the best-selling items here. Unlike OTOP products, yellow oil is produced to be sold to Chinese tourists. Yellow oil is authenticated by the arrival of Chinese tourists, thus authenticity is socially constructed and specifically marketed at Chinese tourists. An Interviewee recounted how Thai tourists do not buy Pattaya Floating Market's yellow oil, as it is expensive for them, and there are many brands of yellow oil. This correlates with research conducted by Pongajarn et al. (2016, p. 11), in which they suggest Pattaya Floating Market connects to Asian tourists while disconnecting from Western tourists. As the interviewees stated, the main target group of the market is Chinese tourists.[4]

ME: Is yellow oil one of the market's products?
INTERVIEWEE: Yep, this is one of the market's products.
ME: Where do you find the ingredients?
INTERVIEWEE: This is our formula, which was created by the floating market. We use ingredients that are well known to Chinese people, as this was the product we chose for Chinese people. This place is a tourist attraction for Chinese tourists, so what is sold here is particularly for Chinese tourists.
ME: Why is this product popular with Chinese tourists?
INTERVIEWEE: This one? It started from green balm, which is popular among Chinese people. We wondered, why? We looked at different colours and the characteristics of prospective users, then we created yellow oil. From our research, we found that Chinese people like green and yellow. Yellow oil is a good-quality product that contains extracts from 108 kinds of herbs. One bottle of yellow oil costs 350 baht [about £7.90], but if they buy up to two bottles of yellow oil, they pay only 300 baht each [about £6.80]. With this strategy Chinese tourists don't engage in price haggling.

(Mr. Nat# n=9# male# Pattaya)

Yellow oil seems to involve two functions: mythological and functional attributes. If it were purposeless, it would become a mere cultural sign rather than an authentic object. Yellow oil is used as traditional Thai medicine, especially for relieving muscle pain, and is a unique souvenir. Its functional attribute, where the frame of reference is the present, does not allow the object to trace back to the origin, but its mythological attribute shows the regression to origin and to the source of value, which are the 108 Thai herbs. It also presents the signature of the product, as it is locally produced by the floating market.

Yellow oil is thus an authentic object, for it suits the preference of Chinese tourists and, paradoxically, has signification of value. The product is split into two attributes so as to strike a balance between these terms, which can co-exist in a complementary way, albeit antithetical. The quest for authenticity, in this way, is the quest for an alibi, or another attribute. What makes the products authentic is not merely functional difference, but rather, a functional attribute needs to co-exist with a mythological one, and authenticity pertains to the play of differences. Apart from authenticity, the socio-ideological function is another thing that makes the cultural contents of Pattaya Floating Market nonessential.

Pattaya Floating Market: a series object

Globalisation and tourism do not correlate with generic cultural content, or what Ritzer calls 'nothing form'. But a place can recreate authentic and distinctive cultural content in tourism. In this section, only Pattaya Floating Market will be discussed.[5] This is because Pattaya Floating Market appears to be a serial form of a floating market, where successive series make the place become a personalised floating market. The place has to water down the floating market's functional essence so as to allow specific differences, or personalised attributes, to emerge. Inessential difference of the socio-ideological system refers to model and series. What follows is a sub-theme that emerged from the interview data.

Modalities of Thainess

Pattaya Floating Market is named the Four Regions Floating Market in order to distinguish it from other floating markets. Specific differences of the place are reflected in its modalities of Thainess.

ME: What is the uniqueness of this artificial floating market?
INTERVIEWEE: With our Four Regions Floating Market, the place didn't inherently become a floating market, as with Amphawa Floating Market, where the local community grouped together to create the market. But [Pattaya] is a constructed floating market, so we knew what sort of uniqueness we would go for from the start. Our uniqueness is traditional Thai houses [called Baan Ruen Thai]. The traditional houses are divided based on the four regions and architectural styles. If we walk into the Northern zone, the style of houses is called Ka Lae. The symbols of traditional Thai houses in central Thailand, the south of Thailand and the northeast of Thailand are called Pan-lom style, Peek Pee-Seua style and Yod Tong style, respectively. Each different style helps divide the market into each regional zone [the North, the South, the Central and the Northeast]. We present this story to tourists so that they know the origins of these symbols.

(Ms. Petch# n=6# female# Pattaya)

In this case, being a four regions floating market is the specific difference that makes Pattaya Floating Market a serial form of floating market. This specific difference does not resonate with the floating market's physical essence, which is tied to a local speciality, not the four regions of Thailand. Being a four regions floating market also refers to 'the whole of Thailand'. The cultural contents of our market are distinctive because the floating market represents the whole of Thailand.

If you asked me whether we have products from the south or the north, yes! We have all the regions' products. We asked tour agencies and they said the tourists thought our place looked like the whole of Thailand. Well, OK, there might be something we missed, but we tried to do the best we could.

(Ms. Nan# n=11# female# Pattaya)

Neither being 'the four regions floating market' nor 'the whole of Thailand' is the floating market's functional essence, instead those specific differences are a successive series of a floating market, where the specific differences enable the market to become personalised. Another personalisation function is 'more than a floating market', of which the following interview gives an example.

ME: Do you think the floating market meets tourist expectations? Because in comments on TripAdvisor, some tourists said, 'The floating market was made up for tourists, but it was unique, so shouldn't be missed'.

INTERVIEWEE: There are two points. Some [of these] tourists saw a simulated four regions floating market, where they could experience the Thai way of life. There were many comments, with some agreeing, while others didn't. However, the floating market has been continually improved/developed. Some thought our place was 'more than a floating market' because it is a learning centre. Our floating market is a learning centre of the local community, where we provide free lessons in Thai traditional art, Thai painting, etc.

(Mr. B# n=1# male# Pattaya)

'More than a floating market' is another serial form of Pattaya Floating Market that operates at the level of a secondary function, or the personalisation function. Pattaya Floating Market is devoid of functional essence so as to allow specific differences to emerge. According to the interview data, the specific differences contribute to a successive series of objects/floating market. Although Pattaya Floating Market is presented as a 'four regions floating market', or 'the whole of Thailand', or 'more than a floating market', these cultural contents are non-essentially different. The place becomes personalised to be different, with the market being able to conceal the fact that there is no specificity in its essence.

With regard to Pattaya Floating Market, each specific difference, including being a 'four regions floating market', 'the whole of Thailand' and 'more than a floating market', attempts to distinguish itself from the others in order to respond to the floating-market model. However, these are only inessential differences. Despite successive series of Thainess, Pattaya Floating Market is anchored in relative differences, whereby the model can integrate within the whole series of the floating market. The personalisation of Pattaya Floating Market seems to conform to the model of the artificial floating market and the code of the tourist-orientated floating market. In addition, a series object also relates to time.

Serial time

Referring back to Chapter 4, model and series are associated with time. Serial time is not enmeshed in either the present or the past, rather it seems to be an immediate past, or an indefinite past, which bears no relation to people who live in a specific time. Pattaya Floating Market engages serial time, with the sub-theme of 'different periods of Thainess' being presented. There are currently three phases[6] in the floating market, as described in below.

> We have traditional Thainess and applied/contemporary Thainess. In phase 2, it shows Thainess in the present. The market presents Thainess in different periods – traditional Thainess, contemporary Thainess and also modern Thainess.
>
> (Mr. Brad# n=10# male# Pattaya)

Moreover, the three phases display different stories of Thainess.

ME: What are the differences between the three phases?

INTERVIEWEE: Phase I represents traditional Thai culture, which took six years to build, while phase 2 displays modern Thainess, which took 10 months to build. But phase 3 has only just been finished [It had been open for three-four months when I was there in 2015.], and it shows Thai culture in the past, such as the Thai riverside culture [the riparian way of life], how Thai people lived in the past. It is built in a very Thai style. All the houses' roofs in phase 3 were made from one kind of banana leaf, called 'Bai Tong Teung' in Thai. Also, in phase 3 there is an elephant camp, an economically self-sufficient village, a fruit garden, an organic rice farm, a monkey show and a boat museum.

(Mr. Aong# n=13# male# Pattaya)

Below is a further description.

INTERVIEWEE: In phase 1, there are old wooden houses, while we have modern wooden houses in phase 2, where there is also an air-conditioned food court. In phase 3, there is a 'Bai Tong Teung' (a banana leaf village) and a monkey show. We also display the ancient way of life when there was no electricity and gas. Our staffs live in the village to show the way of life in the past. I am one of them who has tried living in the village.

ME: Was it hard to adapt to that sort of thing?

INTERVIEWEE: Not really, because I come from the countryside, and this was similar to life in a rural area, which was not convenient.

ME: Which city are you from?

INTERVIEWEE: From Sakon Nakorn [in the northeast of Thailand]. I got used to that sort of life. The village in phase 3 shows the Thai way of life in the past, such as rice farming, cooking rice with clay pots and Thai massage. So in phase 3 you can see both the ancient and local Thai way of life.

ME: Do many tourists visit phase 3?

INTERVIEWEE: Yeah, lots of them! They are able to buy a boat-tour package on our amphibious boat[7] to take them there.

(Ms. Kaew# n=17# female# Pattaya)

Based on the interviews, modalities of Thainess can also be divided into different periods. There is traditional Thainess in phase 1, modern Thainess in phase 2, with ancient Thainess in phase 3. Pattaya Floating Market, as an antique object/ commodity sold to tourists, is regulated by the same laws in accordance with the model/series scheme. The place refers to cultural nostalgia and that different periods of Thainess are serial times. Serial times allow the market to go higher up the ladder of created value in the quest for personalisation, which is regression to the past. These pure series, traditional and modern Thainess, are not located exactly in either the past or the present; instead, they are indefinite past, which the difference is hardly noticeable. Ironically, workers are presenting a time that is not theirs, while tourists who are taking part in an amphibious boat ride enjoy seeing different periods of Thainess in a context and timeframe that they have never belonged to. The serial times are only an established value in order to search for specific difference but are devoid of essentials.

Some staffs live in the traditional village in phase 3, which in fact bears no relation to that time at all. Although the floating market displays different phases of Thainess, such as organic rice farming and a self-sufficient and traditional village in phase 3, the serial times do not differentiate one phase from the others. This is because serial times are not noticeably different, with the floating market simply returning to an old time (phase 1), and an even older time (phase 3), whereas phase 2 shows how modern Thainess does not associate itself with the present. The serial times appear to be ephemeral, where one serial time is produced, and is followed by other serial times to increase value in the place. Pattaya Floating Market turns out to be a model that can be disseminated into several series objects. Only when the serial times are insignificant can they personalise the floating market. But how does the abstractness of difference, together with inessential difference, affect tourist interpretation with regard to Thai culture? We will now move on to the tourist section.

The interpretation of tourists

In order to study tourist interpretation, I conducted documentary research whereby I selected the 30 most recent comments on each market that tourists had posted on TripAdvisor, from 4 June 2015 to 20 June 2015, and interpreted this using content analysis. These comprised comments both from members of tour groups and from independent travellers. We might question whether tourists have any firm criteria for differentiating distinctive, from indistinctive, cultural content. Data on TripAdvisor highlight tourist interpretations of Damnoen Saduak and Pattaya Floating Markets. From the data, tourists regard Damnoen Saduak Floating Market as authentic, which depends on different sources of value.

Tourists at Pattaya Floating Market interpret the market as authentic, while some do not search for authenticity at all. Additionally, unique and generic cultural content can co-present. The following data are examples.

Starting with Damnoen Saduak Floating Market, some tourists interpreted the market as authentic and were impressed by it.

> It was a rich culture in that streets were made of water and the only mode of transportation they had were boats.
>
> (comment no.28# Damnoen Saduak)

> What was unique here was the labyrinth of canals that abounded, along with the market stalls on the sides of the canals.
>
> (comment no.14# Damnoen Saduak)

The tourists were impressed with the unique location of the floating market, namely the waterways, boats, the labyrinth of canals and the market stalls. This might be a different, or an away experience that they were unable to find in their home countries. However, some tourists expanded on this.

> It was like nothing else, and the attractions might be touristy, yet sometimes those are the best things, the floating market had something for everyone.
>
> (comment no. 24# Damnoen Saduak)

> It was an amazing place of business. Got up early to see the best of it. So many boats were going in all directions and the variety of produce was huge. I could not imagine seeing anything like this anywhere else in the world.
>
> (comment no.20# Damnoen Saduak)

Tourists do not see 'being unique' as being opposed to being a tourist attraction, or a place of business. As a tourist attraction, the place can become different and unique. Referring back to Baudrillard's theory, the mythological and the functional attributes of an object can co-present so that the object becomes authentic. Damnoen Saduak Floating Market can offer an away experience to tourists (mythological attribute), while it functions as a tourist attraction in the present (functional attribute). For instance, it is a place where tourists can see a variety of produce, but it is also a place of business, or a tourist attraction.

Some tourists regard Damnoen Saduak Floating Market as being distinctive, and it can relate to any source of value. For example, tourists view the floating market as representing Thailand and vice versa. They seem to match the place with Thailand, incorrectly, or the whole country, when in fact, a floating market has local cultural content that is tied to a specific locality,

Thailand is rather famous for its floating markets, so if you have not been to any floating market, you have not been to Thailand. One who visited Thailand must visit the floating market.

(comment no. 26# Damnoen Saduak)

There were numerous floating market places in Thailand, so I guessed these were unique to Thailand.

(comment no. 21# Damnoen Saduak)

Those tourists interpreted the cultural content of Damnoen Saduak Floating Market in relation to Thailand and Thai culture. The whole country, or Thailand, turns out to be the source of value, or the mythological attribute of Damnoen Saduak Floating Market (a functional place). Thailand therefore becomes an alibi of a floating market. As well as this, what is unique might be the source of value, as suggested in the following comment about Damnoen Saduak Floating Market.

The most impressive thing was that it was 99% ladies doing all the work here, maybe the blokes were unable to stand the humidity and needed to sleep.

(comment no.22# Damnoen Saduak)

Eating Thai food and mango with sticky rice on a boat, from ladies who sold them on their boats, was extraordinary.

(comment no.7# Damnoeen Saduak)

Some vendors were old and admirable.

(comment no. 28# Damnoen Saduak)

Some tourists were impressed with the female vendors who managed to cook Thai food and sell items on boats on their own. Again, what becomes authentic is not inherently found in the floating market itself, but rather the quest for an alibi that is a mythological attribute of the place. The origin of the floating market is Thailand, and the signature of the market is that women are able to do all the work in the market. These are the sources of value that enable the place to become authentic.

Concerning Pattaya Floating Market, tourist interpretation of the place varies according to different experiences. There are tourists who regard the market as distinctive and who do not search for authenticity at all. Some tourists were impressed with the physical place, as seen below.

I visited here five years ago. It was quite small compared to Bangkok floating market. But recently I visited this April, and it is now greatly extended and better than Bangkok was when I last visited. It had a further phase to go, so should be really excellent in another year or so.

(comment no.1# Pattaya)

As stated in the previous section, Pattaya Floating Market is a series object. The place pertains to the personalisation function and specific difference, where the extended phases, or 'the different phases of Thainess' are series. It seems that the series object of the market makes its cultural contents unique. In addition, what impresses tourists is the source of value.

> It was great that I have been to the floating market. It was a good experience. Though the water was brown, you were be able to see how the local people did it there.
>
> (comment no. 15# Pattaya)

> We went with a tour group and did not have enough time to really shop hard. There were so many little stalls and food experiences, you needed to probably give yourself a few hours to wander. There was a cover charge, but it was not much. The setting was very clever, and it was quite a unique experience. I was a bit rushed, but happy with my purchases here.
>
> (comment no.29# Pattaya)

This agrees with Baudrillard's theory, in that authenticity relates to an obsession with certainty, such as local culture and local people, while visiting the floating market enables tourists to see the local way of life. Authenticity therefore is tied to origin, and also means the signature of a work, whereby the setting of the floating market, which includes stalls and food, appears to have distinctive cultural content for tourists. What is more, the quest for authenticity is also the quest for an alibi.

> Photo enthusiasts would love this place, for there were tons of shots you could take and observe their way of life. If you ain't been to any floating market, you ain't been to Thailand.
>
> (comment no.26# Pattaya)

> It was a very nice market in the boat. All the things from the market were for daily use. One who visits Thailand must visit a floating market.
>
> (comment no.30# Pattaya)

Again, the demand for authenticity, or the quest for authenticity that is found in Pattaya Floating Market, lies elsewhere, especially Thailand. Or rather, Thailand, as a mythological attribute, is an alibi of Pattaya Floating Market. Thailand has no part to play here because its social existence should have been displayed elsewhere. Only when the floating market is associated with Thailand and Thai culture does Pattaya Floating Market appear to be authentic, and can the mythological attribute co-exist with the functional attribute.

However, some tourists do not search for authenticity. Rather, they were impressed with the floating market, for they could have fun and enjoy shopping there.

I loved the floating market, the winding boardwalks with small stalls everywhere, and the haggling was so much fun, people were friendly. A very enjoyable couple of hours in an unusual setting.

(comment no.2# Pattaya)

It was a good place for a bargain and for casual shopping.

(comment no.9# Pattaya)

These tourists found haggling enjoyable. They did not search for authenticity, and did not see the place as authentic either. They just wanted to go shopping, see new things and have fun. For tourists, there seems to be no fixed criteria for justifying authentic and distinctive culture. Some of them visited Pattaya Floating Market regardless of authenticity. Their interpretations vary according to expectation and presupposition. However, there are some theoretical points that Baudrillard and Ritzer oversimplify, which will be presented in the next section.

Theoretical discussions

The conception of globalised tourism

With the production of value and the play of differences, Damnoen Saduak Floating Market is global rather than globalised. It recreates the idea of authenticity to meet tourist demand, with the market offering both souvenir items and local produce. The scale of tourism in the market is expanded in terms of product range. In contrast, Pattaya Floating Market is globalised rather than global. Authenticity derives from flows of an idea that was originally created in Japan, seen in the OTOP products available to buy in the market. The idea of OTOP has been adopted in Thailand and presented as Thai authenticity. The difference between authentically Thai and externally authentic is blurred, for local people have internalised the effect of globalisation.

Another degree of globalised tourism in Pattaya Floating Market is the series object, or the modalities of Thainess. It becomes globalised, due to the reproducibility of floating-market culture. Modalities of Thainess and serial times are contrived culture for tourists which do not relate to a traditional floating market at all. But those series objects make the place more personalised and specific than a traditional floating market. In this way, global flows cause the singular difference between the real traditional floating market and reproduced culture for tourists to disappear. Having presented globalised tourism, what follows is the limitations of working with Ritzer and Baudrillard's ideas.

The limitations of Ritzer's theory of the globalisation of nothing

To stress, Ritzer's criteria for differentiating distinctive cultural content from the indistinctive seem to be overdrawn. Social forms with attachment to place, uniqueness, human relations and personal services are 'something', whereas social forms that have no tie to a particular place and are generic, dehumanised and an automated service, are 'nothing'. For Ritzer (2007), social forms without distinctive cultural content, or 'nothing', are compatible with globalisation, while those with distinctive cultural content, or 'something', tend to be associated with glocalisation.

In this manner, authenticity becomes polarised between the global and the local, where globalisation waters down unique local content, whereas cultural content that is embedded in the local is meaningful. 'Something' is similar to authentic culture, while 'nothing' looks inauthentic. Referring back to the floating-market case studies, the places appear to fall into the 'nothing' end of the continua, rather than the 'something' one, as they are tourist attractions. So are we able to establish firm criteria for separating distinctive cultural content from indistinctive content? Is there any local culture unaffected by globalisation? Or does globalisation exist without interaction with the local?

According to the interview data, what becomes authentic varies due to the different interpretations of workers and tourists, for example, Damnoen Saduak Floating Market becomes an original market, albeit having changed to become a tourist-orientated place. It welcomes the arrival of tourists, yet is still pertinent to its locality, as seen in the natural ambience of the market, the labyrinth of the canals, local people, and so on. Pattaya Floating Market seems to be a unique place, for it is the only floating market in Pattaya city, which is popular for beautiful beaches. It is an artificial floating market, but it differentiates itself from other markets by using the concept of Thainess. Globalisation and tourism do not preclude the two floating markets from establishing their unique cultural content. Therefore, we are unable to say that one has more distinctive cultural content than the other. This is because the markets are sold to tourists as commodities. As commodified objects, the cultural contents of the floating markets are not dependent on practical application, but rather sign-value.

The limitations of working with Baudrillard's ideas

In contrast with Ritzer, Baudrillard's theory enables us to understand how objects constitute the system, and we can apply his theory to study the cultural contents of a tourist place. However, there are limitations to working with Baudrillard's ideas. Baudrillard's theory is one-dimensional, and focuses on the influence of objects over individuals.

> Baudrillard elaborates on the ways in which subjects relate to use, dominate, or are dominated by the system of objects along with signs that structure our everyday life. His work operates within the framework of a subject-object dialectic in which the subject faces a world of objects that attract, fascinate and sometimes control his or her perception, thought and behaviour.
>
> (Kellner 1989, p. 8)

It seems that 'the system of objects' produces a causal relationship between objects and subjects, whereby objects impact upon the social life of subjects. Objects determine the subject's perception and action, for example, antique and authentic objects are valuable for the possessor as they might delineate social status and social class. Looking back at Damnoen Saduak and Pattaya Floating Markets, authentic objects and series objects affect people's actions in tourist places. The fruit and crops sold in Damnoen Saduak Floating Market give a sense of locality, while the OTOP products that are offered in Pattaya Floating Market represent the idea of four regional Thai cultures.

However, the social life of people is not necessarily dependent upon the order of objects, as Baudrillard proposes. Subjects, to some extent, reflexively manipulate objects, and in an artificial tourist place, subjects might be able to organise objects so that the place becomes distinguished from other places. As stated previously, Pattaya Floating Market recruits traders and chooses what products to sell to comply with the theme of Thainess. Regarding series objects, there are different modalities of Thainess in Pattaya Floating Market, and workers display three particular different phases in the play: phase 1 presents traditional floating market culture; phase 2 shows modern Thainess; phase 3 turns to the past in order to exhibit the traditional Thai way of life.

Globalisation and tourism do not organise objects in this way, rather the workers reorganise and rearrange cultural objects and put them into that order. Therefore, it is likely that, in this case, the workers organise the order of the objects rather than the other way around. Workers can monitor the system of objects, and in this manner, 'the system of objects' generates interaction between the object and subject, whereby subjects are able to change the order of objects in accordance with their perception and thought. It may be possible to say that there is subject reflexivity. Not only can workers reflexively rearrange cultural objects in the floating markets, but also tourists can reflexively interpret the places.

To understand how tourist performance co-produces a place and the relationship between the subject and object better, we should look back at 'the performance turn' presented in Chapter 3. Larsen (2006, p. 422) states, 'Tourist places are produced places, where tourists are the co-producers of such places and the performers of these places, hence most tourist places become dead unless actors take the stage and enact them.' Tourist performance makes a place exist, and tourists become co-producers of the places. Without tourist performance a place does not become a tourist attraction. According to the data, tourist performance reproduces and assigns different meanings to the floating markets. For example, some tourists see Damnoen Saduak and Pattaya Floating Markets as authentic and unique, while some tourists in Pattaya Floating Market do not view the place as unique, but simply a fun and new experience.

Another limitation is that while Baudrillard attends to the system of objects, he says nothing about the system itself. The system of objects is treated as totality. As Kellner (1989, p. 11) maintains, 'Although Baudrillard describes the system of objects as a system of commodities that constitutes a consumer society, there is little discussion of the emergence of the system of objects in the course of the development of capitalism.'

Baudrillard does not draw out the connection between capitalism and the system of objects. The system of objects works as a system of commodities, yet Baudrillard does not develop how the system of objects links with others, such as the cultural system and economic system. The system of objects may inextricably involve the implosion of economy and culture. Further to Baudrillard, the co-existence of mythological object and functional object in Damnoen Saduak and Pattaya Floating Markets may link with the commodification process.

In order to appear in a context and time that it does not belong to, the mythological object is commodified. Referring to Baudrillard's example, the warming pan in the oil-heated house, the origin of the warming pan is modified and commodified to present it in a modern context. Based on the data, authenticity accompanies vested economic interest. The commodification process can account for the social construction of authenticity, which is not taken into account by Baudrillard. Also, Baudrillard's theory offers us a limited understanding of authenticity, asserting that authenticity is created by the order of objects being juxtaposed with the mythological attribute and functional attribute. However, the interview data indicate otherwise, as seen with the yellow oil sold in Pattaya Floating Market being authenticated by Chinese tourists. In this manner, authenticity seems to be co-produced by local workers and Chinese tourists. The construction of authenticity is both a globalised and localised process. Authenticity is created by local workers and then reproduced by tourist performance. If yellow oil did not suit their preference, Chinese tourists would not buy it.

Conclusion

Ritzer's theory of the globalisation of 'nothing' is insufficient for studying the cultural contents of Damnoen Saduak and Pattaya Floating Markets. His criteria for separating distinctive cultural content from generic cultural content are overdrawn and the globalisation of 'something'/'nothing' is thus a false dichotomy. In order to challenge and highlight the limitations of Ritzer's theory, I use Baudrillard's theory concerning the system of objects. The cultural contents of the floating markets do not depend on practical application, so the difference is not singular. The cultural contents of the places pertain to the play of differences in which Damnoen Saduak and Pattaya Floating Markets are non-essentially different from each other.

Having studied the cultural contents of the floating markets, what are the cultural consequences of globalisation in these places? How does globalisation and tourism lead to simulacrum? This will be elaborated on in the next chapter.

Notes

1 Being a genuine floating market means that the place was not created for tourist purposes. Damnoen Saduak Floating Market was originally used by local people for water trading.
2 OTOP is a local entrepreneurship stimulus programme that aims to support unique, locally made and marketed products of each Thai tambon (local sub-districts) all over Thailand (Thai embassy, 2015).
3 Yellow oil is a traditional Thai medicine that can heal muscle pain. There are many brands of yellow oil popular among Thai people.
4 This is how they begin to reconfigure flows of tourism in the market. Further details of this will be presented in the next chapter regarding activity in the place.
5 Damnoen Saduak Floating Market does not fit in the model/series scheme, as the place does not become personalised. Rather, the cultural contents of the market are either genuine or fake, thus we might not see a specific difference there as clearly as we do with Pattaya Floating Market.
6 Interviewees used the word 'phase' to describe the characteristics of the market. Phase is typically used in Thai language to explain the expansion of the building project. In this case, the three phases refer to different times when the market was expanded, for example, phase 1 refers to building traditional floating market and regional Thai houses; phase 2 refers to constructing top shop zone and air-conditioned food court; and phase 3 refers to recreating tourist spots around the market, such as a traditional Thai village, rice farm, boat museum, etc. Different areas in the market also represent different periods in Thai culture: phase 1 shows a traditional floating market and regional Thai culture (regional house styles); phase 2 presents modern Thai culture, such as shops selling chic and high-quality items (called top shop zone); and phase 3 displays traditional Thai culture, which does not connect to the floating market at all.
7 This boat runs on land and floats on water. It was created and patented by the owner, who is very keen on boats.

References

Baudrillard, J. (1996). *The Systems of Objects*. Trans. J. Benedict. London: Verso.

Kellner, D. (1989). *Jean Baudrillard: From Marxism to Postmodernism and Beyond*. Stanford, CA: Stanford University Press.

Larsen, J. (2006). Picturing Bornholm: Producing and Consuming a Tourist Place through Picturing Practices. *Scandinavian Journal of Hospitality and Tourism*, 6(2), 75–94.

Pongajarn, C., Van der Duim, R. and Peters, K. (2016). Floating Markets in Thailand: Same, Same, but Different. *Journal of Tourism and Cultural Change*, 16(2), 109–122.

Ritzer, G. (2007). *The Globalization of Nothing 2*. Thousand Oaks, CA: Pine Forge Press.

7 Globalisation and simulacra

Introduction

With the play of differences, how is the experience of local Thai culture constituted in globalisation and tourism? This chapter examines the cultural consequences of globalisation and tourism, and looks at the action in the floating markets in order to examine the interpenetration of the global into the local, as well as the adaptation of the local to the global. The argument is that globalisation and tourism lead to simulacrum in Thailand, as seen in the case studies of Damnoen Saduak and Pattaya Floating Markets and how they move away from reality.

Baudrillard's theory on simulation will be extensively used to study the cultural consequences of globalisation. Referring back to Chapter 2, mainstream globalisation theories attempt to reduce the cultural consequences of globalisation and tourism to specific ends, such as hybridisation, homogenisation, glocalisation, McDisneyization, and so on, yet Baudrillard seems to offer more insightful views on the global phenomenon. Despite having been exposed to globalisation and tourism, Damnoen Saduak and Pattaya Floating Markets engage in different orders of simulacra.

The first part of this chapter elaborates on the first order of simulacrum in Damnoen Saduak Floating Market; the second on the third-order simulacrum in Pattaya Floating Market. The third section looks at tourists, while the concluding section presents a theoretical discussion and the limitations of Baudrillard's work. What follows now is interview data.

The first order of simulacrum in Damnoen Saduak Floating Market

This section highlights the cultural consequences of globalisation and tourism in Damnoen Saduak Floating Market. As stated in previous chapters, the relocation of the market to the other side of Damnoen Saduak Canal, next to the main road, was to facilitate the arrival of tourists; the current Damnoen Saduak Floating Market is therefore not the original, it is a recreation of the previous floating market. The local municipality revived the old market here, called Khlong Lud Pee Floating Market, in order to draw a contrast between the old market and the present-day Damnoen Saduak Floating Market.[1] In other words, Damnoen Saduak Floating Market is a counterfeit, and this corresponds with the first order of simulacrum. At this stage, we can see the differences between the counterfeit and the original.

Food

As a counterfeit, Damnoen Saduak Floating Market is not an ancient and traditional place, rather it is only a reflection of a traditional floating market and of local Thai culture, where globalisation and tourism have resulted in recreating a natural reference to the original floating market. Thai food is a must-try for foreign visitors so that they can sample the local Thai experience. Generic Thai food sold in Damnoen Saduak Floating Market appears to be a counterfeit of local culture, which it co-presents using local, speciality dishes. What actually constitutes an experience of local culture is genuine Thai food, with which some tourists are not familiar.

ME: What is a must-try food in Damnoen Saduak Floating Market?

INTERVIEWEE: J'Im Boat noodles and dried rice, or Kao Hang[2] in Thai. Dried rice is a local food that has existed for a long time, like, many, many years ago. Non-local people don't know what dried rice is. We use the same ingredients as boiled rice, but we don't pour soup over it. So, we call it 'dried rice'.

ME: Most tourists don't know dried rice is a real Damnoen Saduak local dish, right?

INTERVIEWEE: Umm, dried rice is broadcast on TV food shows. Dried rice sold in the floating market is delicious.

ME: What food is popular with foreign tourists then? Thai dessert?

INTERVIEWEE: When Farang [Western tourists] come to the market, they don't try local food. What they do is sit in a coffee shop and buy souvenirs. But Chinese tourists like to have boat noodles, dried rice, or Thai desserts. They [Chinese tourists] have the same food as we do. They eat what we eat. But I hardly see Western tourists trying local Thai food.

(Mr. Wong# n=23# male# Damnoen Saduak)

Dried rice is the most famous local food, which Western tourists do not know and will not try, while Chinese tourists try local food as they see Thai people eating it. So what food do Western tourists usually eat when they visit the market?

The Thai food they like is Tom Yum Kung [spicy soup with prawns]. It is the only Thai food they like.

(Mr. Pong# n=20# male# Damnoen Saduak)

Western tourists like to eat spicy soup with prawns, or Tom Yum Kung, which is not a local, but generic. Tom Yum Kung is a counterfeit of local food, but for Western tourists, Tom Yum Kung, which is regarded as a representation of local culture, enables them to experience local Thai culture. Based on Baudrillard, in the first order of simulacrum we can see the difference between generic Thai food and local speciality dishes.

Unlike Western tourists, Chinese tourists will eat local food cooked by floating vendors in the market, such as boat noodles and dried rice. In this way, Western tourists and Chinese tourists have differentiated experiences, in which the former only access a representation of local Thai culture, and the latter experiences an element of real local Thai culture. This may be because Chinese culture and Thai culture are, to some extent, interrelated. As interviewees report, during the reign of King Rama V, this area was allocated to Chinese immigrants, so Damnoen Saduak culture is a mixture of Chinese and Thai culture. The old floating market, or Khlong Lud Pee Floating Market, even has a Chinese name: Lao Tak Lak Market. Although the Chinese tourists are still foreign tourists, their experience is differentiated.

As Baudrillard says, the first order of simulacrum sees the proliferation of signs according to market demand, which in this case is the arrival of tourists fostering signs to be reproduced in accordance with tourist demand. Here, this is the co-presence of generic Thai food, for example, Tom Yum Kung, with a local specialty, dried rice. The sign of the floating market is not restricted to the realm of traditional culture. It becomes arbitrary and the signifier can refer to other signifieds, whereby the floating market not only reflects a specific locality, but also represents general Thai culture. We are able to compare general Thai food with local speciality dishes. This is the first order of simulacrum, where the difference between the counterfeit and the original is sustained.

Activities

Activities in Damnoen Saduak Floating Market also pertain to the first order of simulacrum. Damnoen Saduak Floating Market is popular with both group tours and independent tourists. Interviewees stated that tourists travel to the floating market to see boats and to be paddled around the market. For group tours, on arrival at the market, a tour guide or tour leader leads them to a boat service and those who want to take a boat are divided into groups of four to then ride in a rowing boat.[3] After that, tourists can ride in a motorboat to explore all of the market. The activity sub-theme obtained from the interviews in Damnoen Saduak Floating Market is now presented.

ME: What else do tourists like to do?
INTERVIEWEE: On a boat ride, they can see local fruit orchards and the labyrinth of the canals.

(Mr. Pete# n=19# male# Damnoen Saduak)

Another interviewee noted that tourists not only visit the floating market, but they also experience nature.

They can take a boat ride along the canal to see a coconut-sugar-making demonstration, the fishing areas and the temples. Even when it's raining, I see tourists taking a boat ride. They can be paddled in a rowing boat along the canals for an hour.

(Ms. Wang# n=22# female# Damnoen Saduak)

Not all tourists can enjoy the same activities, as some activities are only available to those tourists who have purchased a private package tour.

If they take a private rowing-boat ride, they can visit a place called Tao Tarn Bang Le to view a coconut-sugar-making demonstration, taste a glass of fresh coconut sugar for free, and enjoy souvenir shopping there.

(Ms. Helen# n=34# female# Damnoen Saduak)

To offer a representation of local Thai experience, the floating market offers a boat-ride service to tourists, during which they are able to view the market's districts, including orchards, the labyrinth of canals, the fishing area, temples and the local wooden houses. Only tourists who purchase a private boat tour are able to access further attractions, including Tao Tarn Bang Le to see a coconut-sugar-making demonstration, where they can spend 15–20 minutes watching the demonstration and shop for souvenirs. Although the floating market does not offer this activity specifically for any target group, the tourist experience is thus differentiated, depending on what package tour they have purchased.

If tourists join the usual boat-ride service, they can view the market's districts. But if they purchase a private boat tour, they can see a greater representation of real local Thai culture, for example, a coconut-sugar-making demonstration. I was able to do this as I had purchased a private boat-ride service from the local hotel where I stayed for one week during the data collection period. I was able to see the tools for coconut-sugar-making and I also tried fresh coconut sugar (which was too sweet and tasted unnatural). I could also see coconut trees there as well as souvenir items. In this way, signs of local culture are co-presented with the floating market in order to offer a glimpse of local culture to tourists and signs of local culture are proliferated to meet tourist demand.

Referring to Baudrillard's theory, Damnoen Saduak Floating Market is the natural reference of the original market. The present-day Damnoen Saduak Floating Market, constructed for tourists, represents local Thai culture with a display of local ambience. Instead of placing the local against the global, as discussed in Chapter 2, globalisation enables signs of the floating market to emerge. The counterfeit Damnoen Saduak Floating Market co-exists with original culture, such as the network of canals, the orchards and the atmosphere of the place. Those activities represent local Thai culture, since they are not restricted to traditional culture, but they can co-present with the current floating market.

In the first order of simulacrum, the difference between the counterfeit and the original is maintained. Additionally, the data further indicate that the existence of the original is dependent on that of the counterfeit. For example, local fruit orchards indicate a local way of life and are not there simply for their own sake. It seems that the local way of life survives on the condition that it co-exists with the current Damnoen Saduak Floating Market.[4] Or rather, on the one hand, the current floating market derives value from being the simulacrum of the original, while on the other, the existence of the original depends on simulation. If seeing fruit orchards was not included in the activities, it might not then become a local Thai experience. Floating-market culture has thus been remade, rearranged and re-transcribed, and activities here are a reflection of the original culture. A significant increase in the number of tourists has given rise to the liquidation of signs, which forces floating-market culture to enter a further stage of simulacrum.

What follows here is the interview data on Pattaya Floating Market.

The third order of simulacrum in Pattaya Floating Market

In contrast to Damnoen Saduak Floating Market, Pattaya Floating Market is not a counterfeit of an original floating market and bears no resemblance to an original; rather it absorbs the features of an original floating market and devours the real so that the difference between the original and the copy no longer matters. Pattaya Floating Market is a copy that bears no relation to the realm of the traditional floating market at all. The series of the Pattaya Floating Market are not restricted to an original floating market. Thanks to the income from tourists, along with the arrival of Chinese tourists, the signs of floating market and Thai culture are proliferated and liquidated.

Regardless of real culture and simulated culture, the place becomes authentic and unique. This facilitates that place to enter the stage of a hyperreal, in which real Thai culture and the simulated version are imploded. To reiterate, 'A hyperreal shelters from the imaginary and from any distinction between the real and the imaginary, leaving room only for the orbital recurrence of models and the simulated generation of difference' (Baudrillard 1983, p. 4). The distinction between the real and the imaginary becomes blurred, which accelerates a liquidation of the real. Pattaya Floating Market has passed from the second order of simulacrum, in which it is a series object, to the third order of simulacrum, which makes the distinction between the real and the imaginary disappear. It is neither real nor unreal; instead, the place is a hyperreal, where only the simulated difference is produced.

The third order of simulacrum sees a change in the structural law of value that refers to a reversal of origin and finality (Baudrillard 1983). Series which were generated from the model, as seen in the second order of simulacrum, turn out to be themselves models that bring about social forms. Connecting to Pattaya Floating Market, a series of the four regional cultures and the whole of Thailand, has given rise to the model of Thai culture. In the third stage, these series become the model that generates other cultural forms. In other words, other cultural forms are diffracted from the model of the four-regional-culture floating market, and of the floating market within the whole of Thailand. The third order of simulacrum is all about the model.

As the model, Pattaya Floating Market renders the capability of differentiating an original floating market from a copy impossible. Pattaya Floating Market is not dependent upon reference to an original floating market, for the place is orientated towards Chinese tourists. The cultural consequences in Pattaya Floating Market are thus principally subject to the arrival of Chinese tourists. This affects the action in the floating market, including food, film-induced tourism and activities in which the floating market offers a simulacrum of local Thai culture.

Food and dessert

To return to Baudrillard chapter, a precession of simulacra is when a simulacrum happens to precede the original and generates cultural forms. In this case, Thai foodstuffs orientated towards Chinese tourists become local Thai culture.

ME: What type of food do you sell?

INTERVIEWEE: We have ice cream, mango with sticky rice and fruit smoothies.

ME: Do you make them all by yourself?

INTERVIEWEE: This ice cream is from a franchise, but we make the mango with sticky rice.

ME: Which type of dessert is popular among the tourists?

INTERVIEWEE: The bestseller for Thai tourists is noodles and some have ice cream. Mango with sticky rice is the most popular Thai dessert among foreign tourists.

ME: Apart from mango with sticky rice, what else do they like?

INTERVIEWEE: Well, fresh durian, coconut and coconut ice cream.

ME: So, only Thai food is sold here?

INTERVIEWEE: You mean here? Yes, we sell Thai food and Thai desserts. But I hardly ever see vendors selling Western food, as only a few Western tourists visit the market. There used to be a food stall selling hamburgers, then it closed down.

ME: Why do so few Western tourists visit the floating market?

INTERVIEWEE: Most Farang [Western tourists] like to visit Phuket.

ME: What about Western tourists in Pattaya city?

INTERVIEWEE: They are other types of Farang who love the nightlife, bars and walking the city streets rather than visiting a place like the floating market.

(Ms. Orn# n=7# female# Pattaya)

Thai desserts that are sold in Pattaya Floating Market are not local speciality dishes, but instead generic Thai dishes that progress from the model of the floating market within the whole of Thailand. In the third order of simulacrum, the cultural form is diffracted from the model of general Thai culture. The traditional floating-market culture hence loses finality. The reproducibility of the floating-market culture that is orientated towards Chinese tourists enables the place to offer a simulacrum of the local Thai experience, and results in the experience of local Thai culture. Another example is the Thai food that is orientated towards Chinese tourists. I interviewed one food trader who sold southern Thai food:

INTERVIEWEE: My restaurant is popular among Thai tourists, but other traders sell food and products that Chinese tourists like. Of the four types of food they like, the most favourite is durian, mango with sticky rice, Pad Thai [stir-fried Thai noodles with prawns] and Tom Yum Kung [spicy soup with prawns]. They come to our market to try those four dishes.

ME: How many shops sell mango with sticky rice in the market?

INTERVIEWEE: I think three shops, one at the front, one in the centre, and the other in the Southern zone. All of them are popular with tourists, as the floating market has organised walking paths for the tourists.[5]

ME: I see! When Thai tourists try mango with sticky rice here, what do they say?

INTERVIEWEE: The taste isn't Thai.

ME: How is it different?

INTERVIEWEE: Chinese people don't like a sweet taste, and mango with sticky rice isn't that sweet. But Thai people love sweet sticky rice.

ME: What taste do Chinese tourists like?

INTERVIEWEE: They like oily, salty and a little bit of a sweet taste. They won't buy the dessert if it's too sweet.

ME: What about durian?

INTERVIEWEE: They don't like the same kind as Thai people. We need to know what they like. What about you? How ripe do you like to eat your durian? I'm guessing you don't like it soft and stringy,[6] but Chinese people like to eat soft and stringy durian.

ME: Oh, that's strange, isn't it?

INTERVIEWEE: No, not at all, because Thailand exports durian to China, which takes many days and, so it's ripe when it arrives. So, the Chinese have just got used to eating ripe durian. When they visit Thailand, we need to find them ripe durian.

(Mr. Frank# n=15# male# Pattaya)

From the interview, it is apparent that the Thai desserts sold in the Pattaya Floating Market are not original local ones, but yet not false either. Mango with sticky rice is a generic Thai dessert, and durian is a Thai fruit, but the floating market does not offer a real Thai taste as it is altered to suit Chinese tourists' taste. For example, the sticky rice sold there is not sweet but oily, making it a product orientated towards Chinese tourists. In this manner, the distinction between the real (locality) and the imaginary becomes blurred. Thai desserts and Thai foodstuffs sold in Pattaya Floating Market turn out to be an original local Thai experience. Generic Thai foodstuffs and desserts precede the local speciality foods of the original floating market, which triggers a reversal of origin. This leads to the reproducibility of the floating market and Thai culture that does not tie in with the original floating market and Thai culture. Another generic Thai foodstuff, popular with tourists, is Som-Tam[7] or spicy papaya salad. I interviewed one boat vendor selling this.

ME: Are there other vendors selling Som-Tam?

INTERVIEWEE: Yes, some vendors sell Som-Tam, but with a different special side dish. I sell Som-Tam with grilled chicken and grilled fish. Other vendors don't cook grilled fish, though they cook fried chicken, but not grilled chicken.

ME: Do you use different ingredients if you cook for Thai tourists?

INTERVIEWEE: Chinese people don't like as strong flavours as Thai people do. Thai people like three flavours – salty, spicy and sour. Most Chinese people don't like spicy foods and sweet tastes, just a little bit sour.

(Ms. Som# n=14# female# Pattaya)

Som-Tam is a generic Thai food that does not have any particular relationship with the original floating market. Som-Tam that is specially made for Chinese tourists also proceeds from the model of the floating market within the whole of Thailand. Again, this is precession of simulacra, which simulacrum precedes the original culture. Returning to Baudrillard's theory, the action of the model preceding all cultural forms is a reversal of finality. According to Baudrillard, the real is broken into miniaturised units and recombined with other references in order for the real to be infinitely reproduced. Thai desserts and Thai foodstuffs sold in Pattaya Floating Market are miniaturised units of Thai culture, and the cultural forms make sense, or become an experience of local Thai culture, only when they accord with the model. They are thus a hyperreal of local Thai culture.

However, Thai tourists may not experience simulated culture in the same way Chinese tourists do. Instead, Thai tourists are able to access representations of regional Thai culture in the floating market, whereby they can have regional Thai food, such as southern food, or have general Thai food with real Thai taste. If vendors cook for Thai tourists, they ask how spicy they would like it. Thus, these two groups of tourists experience simulation of culture differently. Furthermore, Pattaya Floating Market also offers an entire simulational experience for Chinese tourists.

What follows now is a look at how film-induced tourism meets Chinese tourist expectation.

The film-induced floating market

With film-induced tourism, Pattaya Floating Market is further incarnated as a hyperreal of a floating market and Thai culture. As Baudrillard states, messages in the media are selected and coded to represent reality. The media breaks down reality into simple elements so that they can recombine with other differential combinatory signs. Pattaya Floating Market is a place that is orientated towards Chinese tourists because of the influence of the media. Globalisation enables the floating market to select this reality over others, and this pushes the place into further simulacrum. Since the floating market offers a mediated culture, and a falsified construct of Thai culture, the experience of local Thai culture that it offers is a hyperreal.

Film-induced tourism[8] in Pattaya Floating Market is now presented using interview data.

> We promote the floating market by supporting films and the media. I remember in the very beginning we were able to establish a good relationship with China TV, and they showed a programme on the floating market several times during one month so that a high number of visitors could see it. We offered our market as the setting for free. Game shows and documentaries have also used our place as a location.
>
> (Mr. Liam# n=4# male# Pattaya)

The main reason for Chinese tourists visiting the floating market is to see the real location of a famous Chinese film called *Go Lala Go!* The most attractive thing in it is the film's location, where a woman hung a man's name card on a holy tree[9] and prayed that they met each other again. Chinese tourists want to see this. (Mr. Chris# n=2# male# Pattaya)

As a film location, Pattaya Floating Market attracts a considerable number of Chinese tourists.

ME: Are most tourists from China?
INTERVIEWEE: Yes, our place is a Chinese market.
ME: Do they come on group tours?
INTERVIEWEE: Yes, about 70% of tourists are Chinese. About five years ago, our floating market was the film location for the film *Go Lala Go!* Its most important scene is when a man meets a woman under a holy tree [at the back of the market]. Chinese tourists call our market 'Du Lala[10] Market', so our place is associated with a romantic story. [In the film], a boy and a girl who work in China come to visit the market and pray to a holy tree that they will meet each other again. The woman hung the man's name card on the tree. Then they met each other again in China.
ME: So, most Chinese tourists came here after having watched the film?
INTERVIEWEE: Yes, it was free to shoot the film here, so the media could promote our place for free.

> (Mr. Sam# n=3# male# Pattaya)

'Reality tests you according to the same grill; you decode it according to the same code, inscribed within each message and object like a miniaturised genetic code' (Baudrillard 1983, p. 121). In this sense, reality is transcribed according to the code. Pattaya Floating Market appears to be 'Du Lala Market', with Chinese tourists having named it after one of the film's leading characters. Tourists decode the reality of the floating market in accordance with the code given in the messages from the film. Action and cultural forms in the floating market can make sense on the condition that they correspond with the model of the film-induced floating market; hence the place is a hyperreal of the film and accelerates the liquidation of reality, or of local Thai culture that is open to a different combination of signs, particularly elements of simulated culture.

Messages from the film, namely the romantic story, Du Lala and the holy tree, do not present the facts of the floating market, yet they break down reality into simple elements so that those messages can recreate scenarios of the floating market, and present a selection of reality, especially the romantic scenes. Messages from the film together foster the reproducibility of the floating market with a falsified construct of Thai culture, and sustain a hyperreal experience of Thai culture. At this point some scholars argue, as discussed earlier, that film tourism is not the entire simulation, but rather a combination of real and simulational experience, whereby tourists are able to see a real physical place, while obtaining a depicted experience mediated by the film (Buchmann, Moore and Fisher 2010). The floating market is the real location of the film, but what becomes an experience of Thai culture for Chinese tourists is actually a series of mediated messages from the film, not the market itself. Without film tourism, the floating market itself cannot fulfil Chinese tourists' expectations. The miniaturised units of reality and a selection of reality result in a hyperreal of local Thai culture. Mediated messages generate cultural forms in the floating market.

Below are some reviews of the film *Go Lala Go!*

> This film was shot like a US TV show. It blended Hong Kong culture into the location where the film was set, Beijing. It was based on the pursuit of materialism and had no sense of any real Chinese culture. The cast was unconvincing and the clothing design made every single character in the film look like fashion model.
>
> (IMDB 2010)

> Fast camera cuts, bright colours and copious amounts of product placement made it feel like an American TV show. If I did not know it better, I would assume that everyone working in a corporate office in China drank Lipton tea, while talking on a Nokia phone and emailing on their Lenovo.
>
> (IMDB 2010)

There is a cultural double-take here on which I would like to comment briefly: According to the reviews, the assimilation of global culture erodes Chinese culture. This makes Pattaya Floating Market a simulacrum of a simulacrum. Not only does it show a simulacrum of local Thai experience, but also a simulacrum of American culture. Although it is a Chinese film, it presents a simulacrum of an American TV programme. It mixes Hong Kong culture with the film's setting, Beijing. The film facilitates the miniaturised units of American culture to emerge.

When it comes to the use of Pattaya Floating Market as a film location, messages from the film, combined with the miniaturised units of Chinese and American cultures become a selection of reality. As a copy, Pattaya Floating Market does not bear relation to a real local floating market, and the market itself already appears to be a simulacrum. In being used as a film location, the experience of local Thai culture offered by Pattaya Floating Market becomes mediated by the film. The film experience offers a more real experience than the market itself. The film purports to show references to Hong Kong and Beijing culture, but ironically, causes a duplication of an American TV show. However, the film does not relate to real American culture either, and is just a simulacrum. The floating market therefore enters the third-order simulacrum, whereby it appears to be the simulacrum of a simulacrum. The floating market is not the film setting, but the film itself is the location of the floating market. This is a reversal of origin, whereby the action in the floating market is only a hyperreal. As the simulacrum of a simulacrum, Pattaya Floating Market also becomes a deterrence model.

The deterrence model and replacement

When the boundary between true and false collapses, reality is then further liquidated. This makes the ability to access the real impossible, and so the distinction between the real and unreal is irrelevant. Looking back at Pattaya Floating Market, tourists generate a cash flow that facilitates local Thai culture to be liquidated, and this permits a radical law of equivalence and exchange to emerge. Pattaya Floating Market is a deterrence machine, in that the place only offers a simulacrum of the floating market, and thus a hyperreal of local Thai culture.

Globalisation and tourism result in Pattaya Floating Market becoming a deterrent and then neutralised. Again, this causes a reversal of finality, as well as the generalisation of all culture. This is where the floating market becomes globalised. Instead of hybridisation and glocalisation, as discussed in Chapter 2, the interaction between the global and the local leads to a deterrent to accessing real local Thai culture, whereby the experience of local Thai culture is a hyperreal and simulacrum. With the generalisation of culture, Pattaya Floating Market can transmit a condensed experience of local Thai culture to a wider audience. In this case, a wider audience refers to the different seasons of tourists, which does not matter to Pattaya Floating Market at all.

> The high–low season of tourists doesn't really impact on the market because we have other groups of tourists coming to the market, called replacements.
>
> (Ms. Manee# n=12# female# Pattaya)

And in another interview, the following was revealed about seasons.

ME: When is the low season of tourists?
INTERVIEWEE: Foreign group tours always visit the market over the course of the year, but there are some differences. For example, the high–low season of

tourists from the Middle East is different from that of Chinese tourists. Chinese tourists come here all year round. I can't tell you how we do this because it's the market strategy.

(Mr. Brad# n=10# male# Pattaya)

Based on the interviews, the high–low season of Middle Eastern tourists is different from that of Chinese tourists, who are the main customers of the market and visit all year round. Pattaya Floating Market is a place orientated towards Chinese tourists. The interaction between the global (flow of tourists) and local (Pattaya Floating Market) generates a unique outcome that might differ from what happens in other locales, for instance, Damnoen Saduak Floating Market experiences a difference in high–low season. But for Pattaya Floating Market, an increase in Chinese tourists renders the high–low season of tourists irrelevant, as they visit the market all year round. Globalised tourism does not produce a homogenised impact, yet its effect turns out to be deterrent, whereby structural forms of global flow are exchangeable and replaceable with one another.

Simulacrum and activities

Globalisation does not water down the experience of local Thai culture; instead it is impossible to differentiate between the effect of tourism and globalisation and that of localised culture, since the hyperreal associates with a reversal of origin and finality. The cultural forms in Pattaya Floating Market do not only proceed from the model of the floating market with its four regional cultures, and of the floating market within the whole of Thailand, but also the model of the floating market within entertainment. This is a hyperreal experience that is produced specifically for foreign tourists. When I collected interview data in the floating market, I only saw Chinese tourists and Asian tourists participate in the activities of souvenir and food shopping, while Thai tourists only took photographs. When tourists arrive at the floating market they are led to a foreign-tourist entrance, where they need to pay 200 baht (£4.00) as an admission fee. A tour guide then takes the tourists around the market to see the shows and cultural performances, and to recommend what products they should buy. To illustrate the deterrence model, the sub-theme activities of Pattaya Floating Market will be presented.

For foreigners, we have a package tour [800 baht, or about £16.00 per person] of a rowing-boat ride to go sightseeing around the market [phase 1 and 2], then they are transferred to an amphibious boat [which can drive on land and float on water] to visit phase 3, where tourists can see an economically self-sufficient village, a fruit garden, a rice farm, a monkey show, a Thai boat museum and an ancient Thai village with four regional kitchen styles. Tourists can also feed the fish and view a Thai dessert-making demonstration.

(Mr. Aong# n=13# male# Pattaya)

In addition to the package tour, regional cultural performance is also a highlight of Pattaya Floating Market.

INTERVIEWEE: We try to find interesting activities for tourists, especially cultural performances. We are currently putting on a cultural performance of the central region.

ME: Do you have a show every day?

INTERVIEWEE: I'm not sure. For example, on Wednesdays, there's a boat parade at the front and a musical show at the back, or we have a northern-style music performance in the Northern zone.

ME: Who arranges all the shows?

INTERVIEWEE: They are arranged by all of our staff.

ME: How do you know what to do or how to select a cultural show?

INTERVIEWEE: We always change them. We don't want repetition. We need to keep people's attention, for instance, for six months we have a drum show. For the next six months, we might hire other shows to perform here. Before that, we had regional Thai dance performances, such as a northern Thai dance.

ME: So, they are professionals?

INTERVIEWEE: Yes, they're all professionals, especially the drum show. They are our staff, and we have our own musical band. There's no need to be worried!

(Ms. Nan# n=11# female# Pattaya)

Tourists can take a boat-ride service to go sightseeing in the floating market, such as to see the ancient Thai village and the boat museum, or watch regional cultural shows along with a Thai-dessert-making demonstration. The place does not bear any relation to a traditional floating market or regional Thai cultures at all. Therefore, an experience of Thai culture does not represent Thai culture, but rather a hyperreal experience. The most famous activity here is sea boxing, as explained below:

ME: So, tourists can see Thai culture here?

INTERVIEWEE: What we present is a simple thing. We try to bring lots of fun, particularly Muay Talay [a Thai sea boxing show]. Two guys [sitting astride a pole set over water] punch each other until one drops into the water; usually it's both of them. We have a traditional Thai music show, boat parades by female Thai dancers in traditional costumes and an artistic performance. We try to have something different day by day and week by week, but what we most regularly have are a boat parade and Muay Talay. We operate and launch special events and special contests for the Song Kran and Loy Kratong[11] festivals, and so on.

(Mr. Liam# n=4# male# Pattaya)

Sea boxing is regarded as a Thai folk sport and was originally popular in the south of Thailand. But it does not relate to the activities of a traditional floating market or the locality of Pattaya. It is a hyperreal experience when it is presented in the context of the tourist-orientated floating market. Non-floating market culture can thus be combined with floating-market culture. Activity in Pattaya Floating Market is a combination of Thai culture and non-Thai culture, especially entertainment activity. Referring back to Baudrillard, the presence of culture and anti-culture makes culture neutralised, so that there is no difference between them at all, as well as being more generalised, with culture becoming exchangeable with signs of non-culture. It shows how the local accommodates the global. Although there are some activities that bear no relation to Thai culture, Pattaya Floating Market still needs them.

> At the back of the market, we have an adventure zone that is 10 metres and costs 200 baht (about £4.00) for tourists to enter. They can enjoy taking photographs and walking on a suspension bridge to see a view of the market.
>
> (Mr. Aong# n=13# male# Pattaya)

Thai cultural activity is combined with tourist viewing spots, namely a suspension bridge and an adventure zone. These activities are rearranged into possible scenarios of the floating market. They are not references, or representations, of local Thai culture or of the traditional floating market, as those in the first order of simulacrum in Damnoen Saduak Market are. Rather, they proceed from the model of the floating market within entertainment. The activities precede the experience of local Thai culture, whereby they devour real, local Thai culture.

The establishment of Pattaya Floating Market conceals the fact that it is the real Thailand, while indicating all of Thailand is not real, and it also saves the reality principle, that local culture is actually there. Tourists can experience a variety of Thai cultural forms, and in doing so, access the whole of Thailand, as well as the four regional cultures. As we saw in Baudrillard's work on Beaubourg, Pattaya Floating Market turns out to be the space of deterrence that triggers social discourse and cultural manipulation, as seen in the floating market's cultural shows and entertainment.

Cultural activities here are anachronistic, with the incoherence of cultural contents being able to co-present. Or, culture here is simultaneously counter-culture. Pattaya Floating Market seems to be a deterrent to every attempt to access a real traditional floating market, as seen with the display of four regional Thai cultures and regional Thai performances, and in its references to real local Thai culture, particularly the recreation of entertainment activities, such as a fishpond, an adventure zone and a suspension bridge. These activities are not restricted to a traditional floating market or local Thai culture. They are constituted by a differential combination of signs. This neutralises local Thai culture in the floating market. An experience of local Thai culture becomes generalised, where culture is exchangeable with antithetical culture as seen with the floating market and the sea boxing show.

Connecting to Baudrillard's deterrence model, Pattaya Floating Market thus appears to be polyvalent, or a multipurpose space, where culture itself is dead.

The implosion of culture and non-culture leads to a total hyperreality. Pattaya Floating Market is not a simulacrum of the local Thai experience, but just a simulacrum of a simulacrum, where things proceed from the model and are subject to signs. There is no difference between the real and unreal, just a simulacrum and a hyperreal.

Furthermore, the third order of simulacrum in Pattaya Floating Market is sustained by the alibis of the counterfeit in the first order of simulacrum, which are the traditional floating market and the four regional Thai cultures. These alibis do not represent, or reflect, an original floating market or real local Thai culture, as in the first order of simulacrum seen in Damnoen Saduak Floating Market. Rather, they are only the alibis in Pattaya Floating Market because they do not need to function in the third order of simulacrum. Their social existence lies elsewhere.

The only reason they appear in Pattaya Floating Market is to supply the content of the following order of simulacrum. The alibis of regional cultures are the preceding orders that supply the substance of the empty subsequent orders of the floating market. For example, the construction of the four regional cultures gives meaning to the regional dance shows, or the four regional cultures become the model that precedes all cultural forms. Cultural forms and activities are not recreated for culture's sake; instead they are created to assign meaning to the simulacrum of the floating market. A hyperreal of local Thai culture in Pattaya Floating Market deters any attempt to access a traditional floating market and real local Thai culture, with the result that the floating market turns out to be the real Thailand, and the rest of Thailand is therefore unreal.

So how are tourists drawn differently into the simulacrum of local Thai culture? It is to the tourist section that we now turn.

Tourist experience

This section presents survey data collected from two groups of foreign tourists: tourists who have visited a floating market in Thailand and tourists who have not. I conducted the survey in English, with foreign tourists staying at two hotels in the Khao San Road area in Bangkok.[12] Therefore, the findings only show foreign-tourist experiences, not others. I suggest that, to some extent, the interpretation of tourists who have never been to a floating market is similar to those who have been to a floating market.

Referring back to the Beaubourg model, discussed in Chapter 4, spectators come not only to participate in, but also to erase all meaning of local Thai culture. The more they come to see simulated culture, the more the meaning of local culture is eroded. The simulation of culture that is displayed in the floating markets fosters what Baudrillard calls 'the production of the masses'. In this case, the masses or spectators, refers to tourists who come to enjoy and participate in cultural simulation in the floating markets. Local Thai culture and floating-market culture exist in reduced forms, which vary according to the floating market, and this may enable the markets to offer condensed local Thai culture to tourists. Ironically, simulation of culture is the route by which tourists access an experience of Thai culture.

The survey had eight questions, and 36 surveys were completed in total. Of these, 24 foreign tourists had not previously been to a floating market, and only answered the last two questions, which were 'Did you plan to visit a floating market and why?' and 'What did you expect to see in the market?' The data are shown in Table 7.1.

Table 7.1 Survey data obtained from tourists who had not previously been to a floating market

Respondent number	Presupposition	Expectation
1	Yes	Food, shop, shirts.
2	Yes, it looked so beautiful in every paper and on TV	I expected to see fruit, souvenirs and many traditional Thai things.
3	Yes, beautiful area.	Experience and boats.
4	Yes sure, interesting market.	Nature, people.
5	I wanted to see Thai culture, food and have new experiences of the market on the river.	I expected to see Thai people's style.
6	I wanted to see it, but it was too far from our accommodation in Thailand. I had a lot of things to see.	Lots of boats with different sorts of food, a colourful and beautiful place.
7	No, because we didn't have time to do it. The express bus to the market takes too long from Bangkok.	I expected a wonderful market on a river or lake with many little boats with food and stuff. The visitors can walk through the market on piers. I was really sad that we didn't have time for it.
8	Yes, it looked like an experience steeped in culture.	Boat, stalls, spices, food and culture.
9	No, beautiful place and unseen.	A range of Thai goods including clothes and food.
10	Yes, it seemed like an authentic experience. We are sorry we missed it.	General products sold and freshly produced, and the food was what I was expecting. Also, handmade and authentic products from Thailand.
11	Yes, beautiful.	Food and fruit.
12	No, because I didn't have time. Maybe I would go there, I don't know.	Boats and fish.
13	Yes, of course, because it's a traditional place of Bangkok.	Boats, long tail boats, fruit, food, culture.
14	Maybe.	Bags, figures of elephants, food, fruit and clothes.

(*Continued*)

Table 7.1 (Cont.)

Respondent number	Presupposition	Expectation
15	Yes, I had read good reports on the internet about it.	Much like walking the streets but on rafts and long tail boats, many traders and stalls selling things.
16	Yes, a different sight/type of market to see.	I expected to see stalls, food stands, clothes, fruit and the sea.
17	Yes, beautiful.	Food and fruit.
18	Yes, beautiful.	Food and fruit.
19	No, I was unaware of the market as it was not widely advertised on the Khao San Road, and time would not allow for a visit.	I wasn't sure. I had not seen any advertisements.
20	Popular place.	Local products.
21	No, limited time. If we were staying longer, I would definitely go.	Lots of fresh produce, some spices and fresh flowers.
22	Yes, when we return to Bangkok. It looked very interesting and different from what we have back home.	Flowers, food and interesting people.
23	Been told by many people to go there. Heard good things about it.	Many crazy things I didn't get to see back home.
24	No, because I was leaving for France today, but I will return.	Boats, floating vendors, all sorts of things. The kindness of merchants, all those colours and also the boat purchases.

Regarding the column headings, 'presupposition' refers to reasons why they would like to visit a floating market in the future, and 'expectation' means what they hope to see in a floating market if they have an opportunity to visit one.

There were three types of presupposition: first, nine out of 23 tourists said the market looked beautiful and interesting; second, eight tourists had a special presupposition, such as Thai culture, food and a new and different experience from what we experience back home. Third, they had heard about the floating market from the media, such as favourable reports on the internet and by word-of-mouth.

Moving on to the second sub-theme of expectation, foreign tourists were asked, 'What did you expect to see in the market?' Food was the first thing they thought about, then boats, stuff/goods, a market on the river/lake, traders, stalls and culture. Thus, tourists expect to see a variety of Thai culture in floating markets, such as food, boats and products.

For foreign tourists who had not been to a floating market, the floating market therefore signified local Thai culture, namely food, products, an authentic experience, traders, and more besides. Most of them said they would visit the floating market if they had time. Although they had not previously been to a floating market, they knew what they should expect to see at one. In this way,

tourists involve the third order of simulacrum that all Thai cultural forms proceed from the model of a floating market. Only cultural forms that accord with
the model make sense.

Due to insufficient data, it seems impossible to say whether tourists are able
to differentiate real Thai culture from unreal Thai culture, and tourists might
not be interested in doing so. They would like to visit a floating market to get
a glimpse of local Thai culture, and they unconsciously obey the imperative of
a cultural simulacrum. Whether it is real or unreal culture might not matter to
them. Floating markets thus appear to be a way for tourists to obtain an experience of local Thai culture.

I then went on to look at survey data on tourists who had been to a floating
market. In the survey, there were 12 tourists who had visited different floating
markets within and outside Bangkok. They answered questions 1–6. After the
respondent number, there are four column headings. The first is the name of the
floating market; the second is the tourists' perceptions of the floating market
they visited; the third is whether they felt Thai culture was represented in the
floating market; and the fourth column records their impression of the floating
market. The data are shown in Table 7.2.

Table 7.2 Survey data obtained from tourists who had been to different floating markets

Respondent number	Floating market	Experience	Thai culture represented	Impression
1	Damnoen Saduak[13]	New experience.	Not really, because of too many tourists.	Traffic on the canal/river.
2	Damnoen Saduak	Traffic, too many people and tourists.	Yes, by means of Thai inhabitants who sold every kind of product.	Smiles and people sold things along-side the river.
3	Taling Chan[14]	Ladies worked to sell stuff.	Yes.	Fantastic way of selling stuff.
4	Damnoen Saduak	A typical Thai market and how they sold things.	Their products and their way of selling.	Impressed with the variety of products.
5	Damnoen Saduak	Very traditional and authentic Thai experience.	Yes, Bangkok was very busy, however the floating market showed Thailand at its best.	Even though there were lots of tourists, everybody behaved the same way, and was very welcoming.
6	Taling Chan	It was nice to see something different.	Yes, it showed how people made a living in Thai culture.	The items on sale were beautifully made.

(Continued)

Table 7.2 (Cont.)

Respondent number	Floating market	Experience	Thai culture represented	Impression
7	Taling Chan	The market was fun and an exciting adventure.	The sellers were friendly and had a variety of Thai goods and crafts available to buy.	I was impressed with the quality of goods to buy.
8	Ayothaya[15]	Tasted Thai food and smelled different flavours.	Not so much, I expected something different from a tourist market.	Plenty of colours and things.
9	Ayothaya	Taste, flavour and smell of Thai culture.	Yes, local home-made products.	Not so much, I expected to see many more boats like a real market, not only for tourists.
10	Bangkok Old Town (Ayothaya)	Saw the shops and it gave an insight into Thai life – good experience.	I thought so, some of the items sold were locally made and represented Thailand/reflected Thai culture, e.g. Thai clothes/ paintings.	I was impressed because it was different from anything I had seen before. There was also a large variety of things to buy.
11	Bangkok Old Town (Ayothaya)	An insight into the local way of life. Everyone we passed waved and was friendly.	Yes, it appeared to be uninfluenced by Western culture, refreshing to see.	I was impressed. It was small but not too busy.
12	River tour[16]	I thought it looked very nice, and there were a lot of things. I enjoyed the experience of seeing the shops and the items they had.	Yes, the items on sale were similar to what I had seen in other areas of Thailand and Bangkok.	The market was very small but not very busy. I was impressed by that as places in Thailand are often too busy.

Of the 12 tourists who had visited the floating markets, four went to Damnoen Saduak Floating Market, three to Taling Chan Floating Market and four to Ayothaya Floating Market or what they recognised as 'Bangkok Old Town'. One tourist went through a floating market during a river tour. Although the tourists went to different floating markets, their experience of local Thai culture was generally the same. The floating markets offered Thai culture such as food and products. The first sub-theme is experience. How did tourists view the places? The floating markets are equivalent to Thailand: an experience of Thai culture that refers to the way of selling. Three tourists said the floating markets were a new and different experience.

The second sub-theme was Thai culture. Ten tourists thought that floating markets represented Thai culture, especially the Thai way of life, and that Thai culture in the floating market also refers to Thai products. The third sub-theme was impression. Most tourists were highly impressed with the variety of products. From the survey, the interpretation of the tourists who had and who had not been to a floating market was not significantly different. Regarding the foreign tourists who had been to the floating markets, the places turned out to be associated with Thailand and with general Thai culture, namely food and products. Thai culture means the Thai way of life, food and products. Again, what impressed them was the variety. With reference to Baudrillard, the sub-themes of Thai culture and impressions epitomise the imperative of the cultural simulacrum and the stockpiles of cultural objects respectively.

The tourists visited the floating markets to enjoy the place and participate in activities; they knew what they needed to do and to see there, and they went to the floating markets because they thought the places represented Thai culture. If people thought the floating markets were simply shopping places, would they still go there? To some extent, tourists follow the imperative of cultural simulation in order to enjoy seeing cultural objects and to experience local Thai culture, and they might not pay attention to what is real or unreal. Tourists just want to experience something new and to enjoy themselves.

However, these two groups of tourists engaged differently in the simulacrum. Although those tourists who had not previously been to a floating market perceived the floating market in a similar way to those who had been there, the former did not erode the meaning of local Thai culture. This is because they did not participate in any activity, and did not come to enjoy the floating market. They did not become the 'masses'. Only tourists who visit the floating markets and join in an activity efface the meaning of Thai culture. They follow the imperative of cultural simulation further than the tourists who have not visited them.

In addition, foreign tourists who do visit the floating markets seem to enter different orders of simulacra. Despite simulational experience, tourists seem to obtain differentiated experiences. The tourists who visited Damnoen Saduak Floating Market were able to see a counterfeit of the original floating market, and of local Thai culture, because the place is in the first order of simulacrum. Referring to the interview data, Damnoen Saduak Floating Market is the representation of traditional local Thai culture that does not absorb the appearance of the real. There is still a difference between the real local culture and the counterfeit floating market, as interviewees mentioned previously. But tourists may not know this difference. According to the survey, Damnoen Saduak Floating Market represents the local way of life and reflects traditional Thai culture. In this way, foreign tourists follow the imperative of cultural simulation to see the local way of life, regardless of the real and unreal.

Similarly, tourists who go to Taling Chan Floating Market can access representation of Thai culture. Taling Chan Floating Market had once been a real water-trading site in Bangkok. In 1971, following the construction of new roads, the old floating market was closed and, in 1997, a revived market was renewed and expanded by the local authorities (Buasorn, in Cohen 2016, p. 72). Although Taling Chan Floating Market is a representation of the old riparian way of life in Bangkok, the foreign tourists did not see it as reflection of local Thai culture. Instead, survey data indicate they enjoyed seeing new things in the market and they found it an enjoyable experience. They did not even pay attention to what was real or unreal.

By contrast, the tourists who went to other floating markets, including Ayothaya Floating Market or 'Bangkok Old Town', and took part in a river tour, did not see any reference to an original floating market, but rather simulacra. As models, those floating markets generate cultural forms of Thailand, such as Thai products and food. Again, miniaturised units of culture and the recreation of activity render local Thai culture generalised and neutralised. Based on the survey data, foreign tourists who visited Ayothaya Floating Market had a differentiated experience. Cohen suggests Ayothaya Floating Market falls into the category[17] of 'innovative new floating market', a type that caters to both domestic and foreign tourists, is a business enterprise based on artificially created waterways, and features shops, food stalls, restaurants and entertainment facilities (Cohen 2016, p. 74). The floating market is established to recreate the charm and atmosphere of old Thailand and is themed by metonyms of the old royal city of Ayutthaya (Cohen 2016, p. 75). The floating market is recreated as a tourist site, yet decorated like the old city. The survey data show that foreign tourists viewed Ayothaya Floating Market as reflecting a sense of Thai culture and representing the Thai way of life, albeit unreal and contrived. Referring back to Baudrillard's theory, they represent masses who obey the imperative of cultural simulation. The unreal culture turns out to the real, or more real. Those tourists who obey the imperative of cultural simulation engage the third order of simulacrum.

Tourists who participate in activities offered by the floating markets, such as a boat rides, eating Thai food and buying a variety of products, erode the meaning of culture. Ayothaya Floating Market reproduces Thai culture by breaking reality into simple elements so as to allow these small units to be recombined with one another and generate possible scenarios of Thai culture, such as the theme of the floating market and the different location. What is presented in the floating markets is hyperreal and simulacrum that makes it inaccessible to the real.

Regarding the tourist who went through a floating market by river tour, he/she found the market an enjoyable experience as there were many shops and items to see. For them, the market represented Thai culture, for what was sold there is similar to what is found in other parts of Thailand. Due to insufficient data, I could not tell what floating market this tourist was referring to. During river tours, tourists may pass through different floating markets, so without the name of the market I cannot make further analysis. But what can I tell is that seeing the floating market was treated as a fun and enjoyable experience rather than an experience of real and unreal culture. The tourist did not expect to see the real culture other than a reflection of Thailand. In this manner, general Thai culture replaces local speciality. According to Baudrillard, this is a precession of simulacra, whereby the simulacrum precedes the original. What the floating market offers is a simulacrum of local Thai culture.

Local culture needs to be generalised so as to offer condensed culture to tourists, and in order to transmit it to a wider audience. The construction of Thai culture is simultaneously antithetical to culture itself. Culture is not there for its own sake, but rather for inviting the masses to visit. Although Baudrillard's theory has enabled me to alternatively conceptualise the effects of globalisation and tourism, there are some theoretical issues that need to be addressed.

Theoretical discussion

Glocalisation and hybridisation

Referring back to glocalisation and hybridisation discussed in Chapter 2, glocalisation seems to be a tautology of the dualism of structure and agency, where the global happens to constitute the local, rather than the other way around. This causes an imbalance between the global and the local. However, is there a fine line between hybridisation and glocalisation? I do not think that hybridisation and glocalisation would add anything new to globalisation. A hybridised culture needs to interact with the local so that its effect can occur locally. The cultural consequences of globalisation need to happen somewhere, for instance, a Japanese restaurant in Thailand, named Fuji, serves kimchi[18] (Korean food) as a side dish. This seems to be a hybridised cultural form in which Japanese culture mixes with Korean culture. It brings about a new cultural form that is neither culturally Japanese nor Korean, but something in between. It is a hybridised culture that impacts upon the local, or Thailand. In this manner, hybridisation is a cultural outcome that involves a glocalised process. Hybridisation might not be freed from locality, for it needs to happen somewhere locally.

Globalised tourism

Damnoen Saduak Floating Market, which is a representation of local Thai culture in the first order of simulacrum is, again, 'global' rather than 'globalised'. This is because the difference between the real culture and the simulated culture remains to be seen. The presence of tourist activity and some elements of the local way of life, such as orchards, canals, wooden houses and coconut-sugar-making demonstrations, ensures that the floating market meets tourist expectations. The scale of tourism is affected by global flows.

Unlike Damnoen Saduak Floating Market, Pattaya Floating Market, which is a simulacrum and hyperreal of local Thai culture in the third order of simulacrum, is globalised. This floating market offers Thai foodstuffs as well as a falsified construct of Thai culture in film tourism that suits the preferences of Chinese tourists. It is not about the difference between the real local Thai culture and staged Thai culture. Instead, forms of Thai culture are substituted by Thai culture that is orientated towards Chinese tourists. The distinction between an experience of real local Thai culture and simulated Thai culture is becoming blurred. Instead of hybridisation and glocalisation, globalised tourism in Pattaya Floating Market produces a simulacrum. All culture can be sold in the market. Baudrillard states the usual complaint that everything, culture included, turns out to be a commodity, and conversely, that all commodities need a patina of cultural or aesthetic legitimacy (in Sassatelli 2002, p. 522).

Due to the implosion of culture and the economy, culture is commodified, while commodities are aestheticised; and commodities that are aestheticised can be sold in a cultural marketplace. The implosion of culture and the economy brings about the liquidation of local Thai culture. This refers to the 'hyperculture', as discussed in Chapter 4. Pattaya Floating Market does not only offer Thai culture that matches Chinese tourists' preferences, but also non-Thai culture, such as an adventure zone and a suspension bridge. The construction of culture is simultaneously anti-culture, especially commodified culture. Culture is not there for its own sake, but produced to be sold for tourists. Thai culture orientated towards Chinese tourists along with non-Thai culture erodes cultural meaning and makes the distinction between the real culture and the unreal one disappear.

Global flows liberate local culture from its own realm, with it becoming open to a differential combination of signs. For example, mediated messages from a film become an experience of Thai culture in the floating market. This erodes all difference. Cultural forms and action in Pattaya Floating Market are not an experience of the real local Thai culture, but a simulacrum and hyperreal. As the simulacrum, Pattaya Floating Market acts as a deterrent that only distances us from real, local Thai culture. This does not mean that globalisation waters down local culture, instead, global flows cause local Thai culture and anti-culture to become neutralised and generalised. An experience of Thai culture in Pattaya Floating Market is thus globalised, in that the difference is effaced. Although Baudrillard's simulation can elucidate the cultural consequences of globalisation and tourism, there are some limitations to working with his idea.

The limitations of Baudrillard's simulation

Although Baudrillard's theory can shed some critical light on the cultural consequences of globalisation and tourism, some of the data might suggest otherwise. Regarding 'the production of the masses' in the tourist section, in Ayothaya Floating Market one tourist says he/she expected to see more boats as you might on a real canal. The tourist knows the place does not display the real culture, but as a replica it should have been presented as the real place. Real experience, or simulated experience, may not matter at all. However, other tourists who visited Ayothaya Floating Market viewed the place as reflecting the local Thai way of life, albeit not the real culture. An experience of local Thai culture, in this case, depends on foreign-tourist interpretation. The market may simultaneously offer both a real experience and simulational experience.

Regarding Damnoen Saduak Floating Market, it is the representation of the real, local way of life, but the survey data show that only one foreign tourist saw it as a new experience, and not representative of Thai culture, because too many tourists were there. In this way, the tourist did not pay attention to seeing the real local culture, and just saw new things there. In these cases, tourists were able to have a new and fun experience in the floating markets, although they knew the culture was not real. Tourists might not care whether they see real culture or not, as they just want to enjoy and experience a new place.

At this point, we can look at 'the post-tourist' proposed by Lash and Urry. Lash and Urry state, 'The post-tourist knows that he or she is a tourist, and tourism is simply a series of games with multiple texts and no single authentic experience, for instance, the apparently authentic local entertainment is as socially contrived as the ethnic bar, and that the quaint traditional fishing village cannot survive without the income from tourism' (Lash and Urry 1994, p. 276). Lash and Urry believe tourists can exercise agency. They do not have to follow the script of a place, but can interpret and re-read the script. Tourists are not silent. As the data indicate, some tourists do not see the floating markets as real Thai culture; however, they are able to enjoy those places nevertheless. Tourists are thus not passive and silent, and not every tourist becomes one of the masses.

Additionally, Baudrillard's simulation downplays another group of agents in tourism that is the people who invite the masses to that particular place. From the interview data, I would argue that local workers can exercise agency in creating simulation of culture, particularly in Pattaya Floating Market. Workers there play an important role in attracting tourists to visit, putting on activities such as a Muay Talay (sea boxing) show. As stated previously, Thai sea boxing is a combination of a sport and an entertainment. It does not relate to traditional floating markets or the locality of Pattaya, and local workers are well aware of that. This is the prioritisation of one culture over another.

Moreover, my work correlates with previous research that proposes that Pattaya Floating Market connects to Asian tourists while disconnecting from Western ones (Pongajarn, Van der Duim and Peters 2016, p. 11). Simulation of culture there seems to match Asian tourists' preferences. This is because Asian tourists seem to be little concerned with authenticity (Cohen and Cohen, in Cohen 2016, p. 69). But I would state that Pattaya Floating Market reconnects with Chinese tourists. The place chooses to accommodate some groups of tourists and not others. It displays a simulation of culture that matches Chinese tourists' preferences, offering film-generated tourism and Thai foodstuffs that suit their particular preferences.

Workers know that film tourism and Thai foodstuffs in this place do not represent real Thai culture. Thus, Pattaya Floating Market has become popular among one group of tourists more than others. This is because local people have selectively attracted one group of tourists and not others. Winter (2007,

p. 41) proposes, 'With tourism in Asia, which ranges from Singapore to Halong Bay, Angkor to Macau, locations are becoming re-packaged and re-scripted so as to meet the preferences, desires and aspirations of Asian tourists.' Local people are able to recreate cultural content to suit a specific group of tourists, or rather, the local can reconfigure global flows in order to accommodate a specific group of tourists rather than others.

Unlike the experience for Chinese tourists, in Pattaya Floating Market, local people choose to offer regional Thai food to Thai tourists who can access a representation of regional Thai culture in the simulated floating market, despite being a simulation of culture. Local workers play an important role in producing differentiated experiences for different tourist groups. Gotham (2005, p. 321), suggests, 'The growth of tourism pressures local actors to improvise on past traditions and establish new ones to accord with the constraints as well as opportunities of the present.' Globalisation and tourism do not necessarily water down local culture; on the contrary, they facilitate local people in reinventing it. Tourism enables them to recreate culture. Globalisation and tourism affect local Thai culture, though local people, to some extent, can mediate it. Paying more attention to agency in the simulation of culture may enable us to understand differentiated experience in terms of both consumption and production site.

Conclusion

Based on Baudrillard's simulation, this chapter concludes that globalisation leads to different orders of simulacra. This chapter has discussed the cultural consequences of globalisation and tourism, including food, film-induced tourism, activities and groups of tourists. Damnoen Saduak Floating Market involves the first order of simulacrum, while Pattaya Floating Market enters the third order of simulacrum.

Notes

1 For further information about the old floating market and the present Damnoen Saduak Floating Market, please refer to Chapter 5 on the circulation of value and signs.
2 Kao Hang, or dried rice, is rice mixed with chicken blood, fried with brown sauce (palo sauce) and topped with fried shrimps. 'These shrimps makes this food delicious' (interviewee no.4# female# Damnoen Saduak).
3 It takes about 40 minutes for a ride, and costs 250 baht (about £2.50) per person in the case of a group tour. A private boat-ride service costs 400 baht (£6.00) for a rowing boat and 600 baht (£12.00) for a motorboat, and takes one hour, including a stop at the coconut-sugar-making area for 15–20 minutes.
4 Referring back to Chapter 5, the floating market was moved to the other side of the canal in order to welcome tourists.
5 When entering the floating market, tourists follow green arrows that lead them to the different zones of the market, while red arrows take them to an exit. Walking in the market seems to be well organised.
6 Personally, I do not like durian and I do not eat it because of its smell.
7 Thai people usually have Som-Tam (spicy papaya salad) with sticky rice and grilled or fried chicken. There are many different local styles of Som-Tam, such as Som-Tam

Thai, Som-Tam Para (pickled fish) and Som-Tam Sua (papaya salad with Thai rice vermicelli).

8 Please see the appendix for photographs of film tourism.
9 Please see the photograph of the holy tree in the appendix.
10 The floating market was named after one of the film's leading characters.
11 Song Kran (Thai New Year) and Loy Kratong are popular Thai festivals in April and November, respectively.
12 Khao San Road is popular among backpacker tourists, and it is the place where many tour itineraries start.
13 Damnoen Saduak Floating Market is a 90-minute drive to the west of Bangkok.
14 Taling Chan Floating Market is a popular market in Bangkok.
15 Ayothaya Floating Market is another artificial market located in Ayutthaya Province, the old capital of Thailand, and is a 90-minute drive from Bangkok.
16 Pattaya Floating Market is also categorised as an innovative new floating market.
17 Tourists can take river tours around the main attractions in Bangkok.
18 Kimchi is a traditional fermented Korean side dish that is made of vegetables with a variety of seasonings.

References

Baudrillard, J. (1983). *Simulations*. Trans. P. Foss, P. Patton and P. Beitchman. Los Angeles: Semiotext(e).
Buchmann, A., Moore, K. and Fisher, D. (2010). Experiencing Film Tourism: Authenticity and Fellowship. *Annals of Tourism Research*, 37(1), 229–248.
Cohen, E. (2016). The Permutations of Thailand's 'Floating Markets'. *Asian Journal of Tourism Research*, 1(1), 59–98.
Gotham, K.F. (2005). Tourism from above and below: Globalization, Localization and New Orleans's Mardi Gras. *International Journal of Urban and Regional Research*, 29(2), 309–326.
IMDB (2010). *Du Lala Sheng Zhi Ji* [Online]. Available from: www.imdb.com/title/tt1621780/reviews. [Accessed 12 January 2017].
Lash, S. and Urry, J. (1994). *Economies of Signs and Space*. London: Sage.
Pongajarn, C., Van der Duim, R. and Peters, K. (2016). Floating Markets in Thailand: Same, Same, but Different. *Journal of Tourism and Cultural Change*, 16(2), 109–122.
Sassatelli, M. (2002). An Interview with Jean Baudrillard: Europe, Globalization and the Destiny of Culture. *European Journal of Social Theory*, 5(4), 521–530.
Winter, T. (2007). Rethinking Tourism in Asia. *Annals of Tourism Research*, 34(1), 27–44.

8   Concluding remarks

To conclude, an inconvenient truth here is that local Thai culture is a simulacrum, and my book has shown how globalisation and tourism construct a simulacrum in Thailand. Globalisation does not cause the disappearance of local culture, and it is not necessarily concomitant of indistinctive cultural content. Regardless of distinctive cultural content and generic cultural content, local culture can be remade through globalisation and tourism to fit within a new context. Globalisation is a paradoxical process, whereby local culture does not preserve its originality, although it does not disappear. Flows of tourism affect the establishment of local places and local culture, while the adaptation of the local to the global, to some extent, reconfigures the flows of tourism, for example, a significant increase in the number of Chinese tourists visiting Pattaya Floating Market.

This sounds similar to the concept of 'glocal', yet it is not the same. Glocalisation is the mixture of the global and the local, where the dimension of locality can be seen. But to what extent is it a real locality? We might not be able to separate the global process from the local process as they become interwoven with each other, or even imploded. What appears in globalisation seems to be a mere representation of the local and of the indigenous culture. Local people internalise the effects of globalisation and adapt their culture to the changes induced by the flows of tourism. The idea of the local is reinvented in accordance with the diktats of the global market.

I have used Baudrillard's theory to study the representation of local culture in globalisation. The two case studies of Damnoen Saduak and Pattaya Floating Markets exemplify the impacts of globalisation and tourism on the local, and stages of representation, including the circulation of value and signs, the play of differences and the orders of simulacra. Globalisation and tourism cause changes in form, the cultural content of, and action in the floating markets.

To exist in globalisation, the two floating markets must, inevitably, engage in cultural simulation, which is fed by the economic exchangeability of tourism. The establishment of the floating markets depends on unequal flows of money between the global and the local. People need the floating markets because they are able to make money from them, and use-value and exchange-value are only the legitimisation of commodity sign-value. In this case, globalisation that is associated with the circulation of value and signs is the reflection of the implosion of economy and culture.

Due to the operation of value and signs, there are no specific criteria that differentiate distinctive cultural content from generic cultural content. Ritzer's criteria are insufficient for studying the complexity of globalisation. In order to challenge Ritzer, Baudrillard's theory on the system of objects has been employed. The cultural contents of the floating markets are inessentially different from each other. The places engage the play of differences, which makes the places attractive to visitors but become inessentially different from each other.

Inessential difference between one floating market and another one results in a simulation of local Thai culture and orders of simulacra. The cultural consequences of globalisation and tourism condition action in the floating markets, with Damnoen Saduak Floating Market engaging the first order of simulacrum. Action in the place can represent a traditional floating market, meaning the place becomes a counterfeit of local Thai culture. In contrast to Damnoen Saduak Floating Market, Pattaya Floating Market engages the third order of simulacrum, and it turns out to be the hyperreal of local Thai culture, with other parts of Thailand not being real.

Simulation can recreate local culture so that it fits into the context of tourism. What appears as local Thai culture in Damnoen Saduak and Pattaya Floating Markets is neither real nor unreal, just a representation and a simulation, respectively. Regardless of the real and unreal, globalisation and tourism sustain the idea of the local. With the flows of tourism, traditional Thai culture comes to life. Tourists also find the floating markets acceptable, as they can enjoy what the markets offer them.

The concept of 'globalised tourism' and the contribution to existing knowledge

As discussed earlier, this term is different from 'global tourism', in that global tourism stresses the interrelatedness of globalisation and tourism, and the expansion of the scale of tourism entailing the movement of people, flows of capital and flows of images and ideas. Instead of 'global tourism', I suggest the term 'globalised tourism' to highlight the effect of globalisation on tourism in a local place, which in this case is Damnoen Saduak and Pattaya Floating Markets. I have used Baudrillard's idea to develop this concept. Tourism in each floating market becomes globalised on the condition that the distinction between the real and contrived culture becomes blurred. This concept also shows the implosion of the economy and culture, whereby culture is commodified and produced to be sold to tourists, while tourist products are aestheticised. In this way, tourism that is globalised involves the implosion of the economy and culture, not just economic or cultural reductionism in globalisation, or in tourism.

The floating markets are not entirely globalised and they are globalised differently, with Pattaya Floating Market having become more globalised than Damnoen Saduak Floating Market. This is because the difference between real Thai culture and simulated culture that is orientated towards Chinese tourists has collapsed. Simulated culture has even become an experience of Thai culture in this floating market. In contrast, Damnoen Saduak Floating Market is globalised when it is subject to economic exchange-value and sign-value that make the use-value of the market replaceable.

The concept of 'globalised tourism' can enrich tourism and globalisation studies, in that it focuses on the effect of globalisation on tourism in a local place rather than the interconnectedness of the global and tourism. I have not found the term 'globalised tourism' in the existing literature. Much of that literature uses 'global tourism', and 'globalisation of tourism', or looks at the disadvantages of global tourism on a local place. 'Globalised tourism' enables us to see how a local place implodes into the global flow. To employ this concept more widely, further research is needed.

The limitations of working with Baudrillard's theory

Although Baudrillard's theory has enabled me to critically study the effects of globalisation and tourism, there are some issues that are overestimated. For Baudrillard, there is no longer representation in hyperreality. 'Hyperreality emerges when culture no longer refers to social reality, and hyperreality as well as hyperreal culture marks the end of representation, for representation does not reflect reality, but rather becomes reality itself' (King 1998, p. 94). As discussed previously, the third order of simulacrum witnessed in this research saw simulation and hyperreal culture in which the origins of reality are reversed. Hyperreality is not the same as representation. The real remains to be seen in representation, while the hyperreal absorbs the real and become the real itself. A simulacrum of reality replaces real, original culture, such as Thai foodstuffs and film tourism in Pattaya Floating Market. These two do not relate to a traditional floating market and general Thai culture, rather they are orientated towards Chinese tourists.

But in what sense hyperreality produces the end of representation is still unclear. As arguably discussed earlier, a film-tourism experience may juxtapose with real experience and simulational experience, since tourists are able to see the real physical place and depicted scenes from the film (Buchmann, Moore and Fisher 2010). Tourists need to travel in order to see the real place and achieve the film experience. Film tourism inherently embeds itself in a local place, albeit through mediated messages. In the case of Pattaya Floating Market, workers know that film tourism is a supplement to the floating market, yet inherently local. For Chinese tourists, despite their experience being mediated by the film, they can see the real, physical place. So, hyperreal culture may not lead to non-representation but rather something in between.

In addition, another significant limitation is that the role of agents in producing and reproducing culture is under-theorised. To reiterate, it is evident that Baudrillard ignores agency where subjects are subordinated to signs, the system of objects and simulation. Baudrillard appears to have a one-sided view on structure. My book has a limited understanding of tourism and the social life of the local markets, for much attention has been given to signs and simulation. To understand this better, we should study local markets by looking back at 'the performance turn', as discussed in Chapter 3. For example, Larsen (2008, p. 31) argues that 'everyday routines and habitual dispositions can influence tourism performances, with many of them revolving around pleasant sociality with co-travelling significant others'. Everyday practices affect tourism performances whereby the home experience of tourists always travels with them, such as socialising with significant others at a distance and reuniting with significant others.

The limitations of the data

Relying on TripAdvisor accounts does not allow me to elaborate in detail on the differentiated experiences of the floating markets for different tourist group-ings. Nationality is not identifiable in the TripAdvisor comments. I am unable to differentiate their perceptions, interpretations and experiences on the basis of their nationalities and backgrounds, although the data show some differenti-ations, such as interpretation of authenticity. Regarding the survey data, they only show Western tourists' experiences of floating markets, thereby excluding other non-English-speaking tourists, since I conducted the survey in English.

To study experiences of floating markets of different tourist groupings, further research needs to be conducted with non-English-speaking tourists in different languages. The data obtained from different groups of tourists can be used for comparative analysis. Looking back at the literature review chapter, studying tourist performance, as in works by Larsen (2008) and Edensor (2001), may enable us to see how a tourist place is reproduced. In this case, 'the perform-ance turn' may investigate how differentiated experiences of the floating mar-kets of different tourist groupings can reproduce the places. This might well be of interest to future research.

Moreover, the workers in the two floating markets came from different back-grounds. In Damnoen Saduak Floating Market, most workers were local people, except for the tour guides who accompany tourists from Bangkok. There were three groups of local people in Damnoen Saduak Floating Market, and their groups are dependent on the boat services that they work for. In Pattaya Float-ing Market, all the workers are staff who are hired by the Pattaya Four Regions Floating Market Company Limited, which belongs to a private owner. Some say the different backgrounds of interviewees might have affected the data, however, within the limited timeframe of my research, the two case studies of the floating markets are realistic.

Implications

Based on Baudrillard's concept, globalisation refers to the implosion of the economy and culture, contributing to a significant change in contemporary society. From the data, packages of Thainess and Thai culture are produced, sold and aestheticised in the two different floating markets. The main themes of this book, the circulation of value and signs, the play of differences and simulacrum, implicitly reflect the implosion of the economy and culture. What is culturally produced in Damnoen Saduak and Pattaya Floating Markets simultaneously serves the purpose of the economy and vice versa.

Flows of capital precede globalisation and tourism, and income from tourists, along with the arrival of tourists, affects the establishment of Damnoen Saduak and Pattaya Floating Markets. The economic system, to some extent, regulates the relationship between the global and the local. Flows of capital facilitate the circulation of value and signs and vice versa. Or rather, the implosion of the economy and culture has influenced forms of the floating markets. In this way, it is apparent that Baudrillard undervalues agency being subordinated to structure, although it does not mean structure is an influence over agents, or subjects. It is not as simple as that.

Instead, the pre-established systems predominate over both structure and agency. According to Kellner (1989, pp. 27–28), 'Baudrillard assumes all needs, or use-values, are entirely produced and controlled by the system of the consumer society, whereby he rejects all human agency and creativity'. Needs and desire of subjects are regulated by the economic system, with the consumer society being interrelated with the capitalist economy. In this manner, it is the pre-established systems that control both structure and agency.

The implosion of the economy and culture also triggers complexity of representation in the local places, whereby Damnoen Saduak and Pattaya Floating Markets can reinvent packages of Thai culture. The arrival of tourists does not only economically benefit the places and Thailand but also helps the places and the country to produce and retain the distinctive value of uniqueness, exoticness and authenticity. The two floating markets do not offer free time to tourists, conversely tourists have to pay local workers to spend free time in the markets. The free time of tourists is subject to the law of exchange-value, while the skills of local workers are regulated by tourist demand. Both tourists and local workers are therefore 'constrained labour' in globalisation and tourism.

Globalisation and tourism create cultural simulation and orders of simulacra in Thailand, but this does not have anything to do with a previous authenticity. It does not mean authenticity exists in Thai culture before tourism. Simulation does not make authentic culture disappear; instead, authenticity can be a simulacrum. The cultural contents of the floating markets, as well as activity in the places, do not inherently happen, they are socially and mutually constructed in globalisation. In this way, authenticity is also socially created, which is the search for value. What appears as authentic depends on the source of value, whereby cultural simulation can add value to a place, or an object as well. For instance, Pattaya Floating Market is an authentic place that offers a film-induced tourist experience and also a variety of Thai cultural shows.

Because of globalisation and simulation, we may question whether or not local culture is an alternative to global flows. Concerning the orders of simulacra, Damnoen Saduak Floating Market does not display original culture, it is just a reflection of the original floating market. Here, original culture co-exists with a tourist-orientated one, such as local Thai food and general Thai food, whereas a hyperreal and simulacrum of Thai culture in Pattaya Floating Market cause local Thai culture to be neutralised and generalised. The floating market becomes the real Thailand and generates forms of Thai culture, which is a reversal of finality. Pattaya Floating Market creates a hyperreal of local Thai culture for tourists, for example, a film-induced place, cultural shows and tourist-orientated Thai food. Global demand affects an experience of local Thai culture along with action in the floating markets.

Globalisation and tourism facilitate the recreation and re-packaging of Thai culture and Thainess in the two different floating markets. Simulated local culture seems to match tourist expectation and local people are able to adapt to, or internalise, the cultural consequences of globalisation. Hence, there might be no clear boundary between the global and local anymore, rather they become interwoven with each other. Or rather, the global and the local become imploded. Thanks to the simulation of local culture and globalisation, the difference between the global and the local becomes blurred and irrelevant.

Baudrillard's concept of simulation enables us to examine a significant change in society and to conceptualise the complexity of representation, yet he might be too pessimistic about the fate of simulation when he denies the existence of reality. Cultural simulation makes Damnoen Saduak and Pattaya Floating Markets transmit Thai culture to wide audience. Likewise, cultural simulation apparently enables tourists to get a glimpse of local Thai culture. Therefore, what is the problem with simulation? Do people really search for reality?

There might not be a problem with this, and a quest for the real culture might not be that important. The diktats of the market and flows of tourism foster cultural simulation, which triggers changes in local culture. But paradoxically, simulation turns out to be something that is acceptable for people, as they are willing to participate in cultural simulation. It seems to be a win–win situation for workers and tourists despite a hyperreal and a simulacrum. Workers and tourists both derive benefits from cultural simulation. In order to attract tourists, local workers need to select some parts of their culture at the expense of others, and this may enliven local culture. Globalisation and tourism do not correlate with the disappearance of local culture. Instead, local culture is intentionally recreated by local people, and well arranged in the floating markets.

Regarding tourists, they know the floating markets represent made-up culture, and yet they still think the places are worth visiting. Indeed, Lash and Urry (1994) assert tourists do this playfully. Tourists know local places are contrived and set up for tourist purpose, but they find them enjoyable and acceptable. They just want to visit a new place and have fun. Instead of presenting and searching for reality and originality, local people, along with tourists, seem to accept simulation as a part of society and everyday life. It therefore appears that people enjoy living in the age of simulation.

Future research and suggestion

In order to further understand simulation of culture in the context of Thailand, future research may look at other cultural spaces, namely, department stores, restaurants, cafes, street food and temples. From this, we would be able to see how these cultural spaces engage simulation and produce cultural value. Differentiated experiences of simulation of culture for Thai and foreign tourists could be used for comparative analysis. Additionally, future research on floating markets in Thailand could use photo-elicitation as a research technique, so that we can understand the appearance of the markets on the tourist stage and their representations.

In the case of Baudrillard, future sociological research should pay more attention to his work in capturing social change in contemporary society, especially systems of simulation at both macro and micro levels. This is because systems of simulation and of signs appear to be a totality of which we are unaware. We accept simulation to be a part of contemporary society, with it constituting our everyday life. Baudrillard does not overreact to social changes and is not unrealistic. What he is trying to do is bring hidden facts that receive little attention to the fore.

References

Buchmann, A., Moore, K. and Fisher, D. (2010). Experiencing Film Tourism: Authenticity and Fellowship. *Annals of Tourism Research*, 37(1), 229–248.

Edensor, T. (2001). Performing Tourism, Staging Tourism: (Re)producing Tourist Space and Practice. *Tourist Studies*, 1(1), 59–81.

Kellner, D. (1989). *Jean Baudrillard: From Marxism to Postmodernism and Beyond*. Stanford, CA: Stanford University Press.

King, A. (1998). *Baudrillard's Nihilism and the End of Theory*. [Online]. Available from: https://core.ac.uk/download/pdf/12825875.pdf [Accessed 25 October 2019].

Larsen, J. (2008). De-Exoticizing Tourist Travel: Everyday Life and Sociality on the Move. *Leisure Studies*, 27(1), 21–34.

Lash, S. and Urry, J. (1994). *Economies of Signs and Space*. London: Sage.

Index

Printed in the United States
by Baker & Taylor Publisher Services